The History of Hiram Holliday

Ian Dickerson

BearManor Media

Orlando, Florida

The History of Hiram Holliday
© 2021 Ian Dickerson. All Rights Reserved.

No portion of this publication may be reproduced, stored, and/or copied electronically (except for academic use as a source), nor transmitted in any form or by any means without the prior written permission of the publisher and/or author.

Published in the USA by
BearManor Media
1317 Edgewater Dr. #110
Orlando, FL 32804
www.BearManorMedia.com

Softcover Edition
ISBN: 978-1-62933-775-3

Printed in the United States of America

Table of Contents

Acknowledgements	ix
Introduction	xiii
Chapter One: Who is Hiram Holliday?	1
Chapter Two: The Early Adventures of Hiram Holliday	15
Chapter Three: The Return of Hiram Holliday	25
Chapter Four: The Episodic Adventures of Hiram Holliday	61
Chapter Five: The Afterlife of Hiram Holliday	143
Appendix One: Pilot Script	147
Appendix Two: The Adventure of the Treasure Trove	199
Index	243

This one's for Andrew, Carolyn, Hannah, Jenna and Sara – different kinds of heroes.

Acknowledgements

This book would not have been written without Ben Ohmart, the man behind BearManor and the man whose connection with the Rapp family provided much of the source material for this volume. He's written a biography of Phil Rapp and it's a worthwhile read for any students of old film, TV and radio shows. Indeed, if you just like good books you should also check it out. In fact, whilst you're at it, check out the BearManor website, for they publish a heck of a lot of good books.

Jenifer Burkett and Anthony Powell were remarkably kind and forthcoming about the life and times of their father Richard. And the kindness of Michael and Janine Gallico is also much appreciated.

Martin Grams remains an inspiration and a great help.

"Tired of hard-talking, level-headed heroes? Then meet a new kind. He's soft-spoken, bespectacled Hiram Holliday. But don't let his timid manner fool you, he's a hero alright! You'll agree when you see his dizzy adventures."

"He's television's most refreshing hero, played by television's most refreshing personality, Wally Cox. Hiram's adventures are a unique, entertaining blend of thrills and laughs."

TV ads for *The Adventures of Hiram Holliday*

Introduction

Fictional heroes come in all shapes and sizes. Some, like the deductive genius Sherlock Holmes, the buccaneering Simon Templar or the blunt instrument that is James Bond, seem immortal, destined to be periodically revived and rebooted. Others though, like Hiram Holliday, are not so lucky and seem to be overlooked and forgotten. Until now.

The alliterative Mr Holliday was the hero of a small number of short stories and books written by noted American author Paul Gallico, though for a generation of people he was also the hero of a short lived TV series—based on those stories--which initially aired in the US in the late 1950s, a few years later in the UK and subsequently around the world. For people of a certain generation it generates fond memories, but being of a certain vintage —and committing the 21st century sin of being in black and white--the show hasn't been rebroadcast in decades and with just a small handful of episodes available online it's rapidly becoming a faded memory. Until now.

This was a TV show, the pilot for which scored higher in test viewings than shows with future TV legends Johnny Carson and Phil Silvers. This was a show with an established and popular star as its lead that everybody liked—it should have had a long run. When the BBC in the United Kingdom aired it—at a time when there were just two TV channels competing for audiences—his adventures were popular enough to get a repeat run just a few months later. Such a quick repeat was almost unheard of at the time for an imported show. Yet this was a show that got pulled off its initial American network before the end of its run, with a sponsor prepared to take a sizeable financial hit rather than air further episodes.

What happened?

Come now, and discover the amazing adventures of Hiram Holliday...

Chapter One: Who is Hiram Holliday?

Meet Hiram Holliday.

He is, according to a description early on in the first story, a "stoutish little man...with unruly sandy hair and bright blue eyes behind steel-rimmed spectacles". 'Unremarkable' would appear to be an apt description. Indeed just a few paragraphs later another character, observing Hiram, asks her companion, "Did you ever see a duller-looking man?"

But Hiram has a secret...

"What no one knew was that outside office hours Hiram Holliday was a gentleman adventurer; that laboriously, with infinite pains and patience, he had in his later years acquired all the outward attributes of the romantic hero...He learned to do the things that make men men, many old things that they had to do to survive... He went to fencing *salle* and shooting school and took lessons in foil, epee and sabre, pistol and rifle...Laboriously, an hour a week, because it was all he could afford, he mastered the art of flying a plane. He joined the National Guard and drilled once a week. He went to a gymnasium and learned to box, and even acquired a smattering of ju-jitsu. These were the escapes...which gave him the zest for living."

He first appeared in a series of short stories *Cosmopolitan* magazine in 1939. Written by Paul Gallico they were quickly collected into book form and published later that same year—his first published work of fiction. Nowadays Gallico is best remembered for his book *The Snow Goose*, about the relationship between a hunchback and a young girl, or perhaps his novel *The Poseidon Adventure*, which was later adapted into the 1972 film of the same name but he was a prolific writer and spent a lifetime working as a storyteller.

Paul William Gallico was born in a Park Avenue boarding house in New York City at four thirty in the morning of July 26th, 1897. His father was Paolo Gallico, a well-known pianist and composer. Gallico Senior was born in Trieste, Italy in May 1868 and had first come to America at the age of fourteen when he made his first appearance as a concert pianist in New York City. He returned around a decade later as a solo pianist with a number of leading symphony orchestras. He met and married Hortense Erlich, an Austrian lady, and when they came to New York in 1895 he set himself up as a music teacher to help provide a regular income. One of his pupils was Jerome Kern, who would go on to become one of the leading musical theatre composers of his day.

Gallico Junior was a small, weak, sickly child and had a governess to take him to school until he was ten years old. Those physical issues perhaps help explain why one of his early boyhood ambitions was to be a doctor, for when he was at camp he carried a first aid kit with him and would bandage the other kids when they were hurt. Another boyhood ambition, perhaps unsurprisingly, was to be a writer.

He attended PS 6 and PS 70 in New York before moving on to DeWitt Clinton High School and graduated from there to enter Columbia University in 1916. But with World War I in full swing he took time out from his education and enlisted in the US Naval Reserve. Because of his poor eyesight he initially attained, as he put it, "the loathsome rating of yeoman". He did manage to progress to become a gunner's mate, however he later confirmed that the nearest he came to seeing service was watching a French liner bound for France from a nearby ferry.

After the war he returned to university and worked his way through a number of jobs to pay his tuition fees including stints as a tutor, translator, longshoreman, an usher at the Metropolitan Opera, librarian, gymnasium attendant and a factory hand. He was also a keen rower and in his final year, captain of the university crew with many press reports calling him "the most powerful rower in the boat". He graduated from Columbia University with a Bachelor of Science degree in 1921.

That same year he married his first wife, Alva Taylor, the daughter of a *Chicago Tribune* columnist and started work as the review secretary for the National Board of Review of Motion Pictures, an organisation dedicated to selecting and discussing what its members regard as the best films of the year. But it wasn't what he was looking for and just a few months later he joined the *New York Daily News* as film critic. However, within a year he was moved to the sports department for, as he would later confess, "being too fresh".

Sports would prove to be his niche. In August 1923 he was assigned to cover Jack Dempsey, the world heavyweight boxing champion, who was preparing to defend his title against Luis Firpo and was at a training camp in Saratoga Springs in New York.

"My burning curiosity got the better of prudence," Gallico later wrote. "I presented myself to Dempsey one August afternoon on the porch of his cottage at the camp and asked whether he would spar a round with me so that I might write a story on how it felt to be hit by an expert." It was arranged for the following Sunday. "I'd never had gloves on before, it was a sheer experiment," he would later recount. With 3,000 spectators on hand, "I can remember seeing Dempsey's berry-brown arm flash for one instant before my eyes. Then there was this awful explosion within the confines of my skull, followed by a bright light, a tearing sensation and then darkness. Slowly it grew light again. I was sitting on the canvas with one leg folded under me, my mouth bleeding, grinning foolishly. The ring made a clockwise revolution, stopped, and then returned with a counter clockwise movement…And, like an idiot, I got up!"

He lasted one minute and thirty-seven seconds.

"I was assisted from the enclosure and taken someplace else to lie down until my addled wits collected themselves sufficiently for me to get to my typewriter. I had a splitting headache and was grateful to be alive."

That experience with boxing lead to other challenges: golfing against Bobby Jones, swimming with Johnny Weissmuller and trying to get a hit off Dizzy Dean. He also raced cars and boats and flew aeroplanes. About a year later he was made sports editor on the paper and for the next thirteen years, seven days a week he was allowed to think, write and say what he pleased in his own daily sports column.

Early in 1936, having sold a short story for $5,000, he made the decision to give up sports writing, go freelance and write fiction. "I was scared to death," he told *The Los Angeles Times* in a 1972 interview. He'd sold a number of short stories to the *Saturday Evening Post* whilst still working as sports editor on a rival publication and "in one of those lucid moments of self-analysis that are sometimes given to us, it seemed to me I had tarried long enough by the wayside. It was then or never."

He retired from sports writing, went to live in Europe and never looked back.

He later confessed to *New York Magazine*, "I'm a rotten novelist. I'm not even literary. I just like to tell stories and all my books tell stories…And before I fold up, I hope to write stories that are better than the stories I've written…I'll write as long as my brain is able to put two sentences together." He went on to write and sell short stories, articles, novelettes and serials to magazines such as *Cosmopolitan, Colliers, The American Magazine, Good Housekeeping, Liberty, Esquire, Reader's Digest* and the *New Yorker*.

Whilst *The Adventures of Hiram Holliday* was published in both the US and the UK in 1939, its origins lie in the Autumn of 1938 when, arriving in London, he received a telegram from *Cosmopolitan* magazine asking if he would do a tour of the six major cities of Europe—London, Paris, Berlin, Prague, Vienna and Rome—with a view to gathering background material for a series of short stories that would combine reporting of conditions, people and their emotions in those cities. In his book *Confessions of a Storyteller*, published in 1961, he elaborated:

> "Hiram Holliday was born in a Dutch K.L.M. transport plane, en route between Hanover and Berlin, sketched on the backs of envelopes, and developed and completed in the Adlon Hotel shortly after arrival. The name was carefully composed. 'Holliday' has a dashing, attractive ring to it. Everyone likes the word 'holiday.' It makes us think of gay, carefree times when exciting things can happen to us. 'Hiram' is a country name, simple, naive, and rooted in the American soil. Hiram Holliday had a rhythm to it that caught on. The character was as carefully thought out and put together. I was after a new kind of reader-identification. It seemed to me that the clients of the magazine must be tiring of the superperfection of the muscular and invincible hero. I wanted to offer a figure not only with whom the average man past his youth could identify himself in spirit but whom he could actually see himself matching in physical prowess, without too much stretching of the imagination. If Hiram Holliday, a sedentary ex-copyreader and a rank amateur at such dramatic avocations as fencing, riding, shooting, flying, swimming, judo, and skiing could be a kind of d'Artagnan, adventuring around tortured Europe—well, who couldn't?"

Who Is Hiram Holliday?

The first adventure for Hiram was entitled 'Crisis in London' and appeared in the March 1939 edition of the magazine. Gallico later recalled,

> "'Crisis in London' was written in Cuernavaca, Mexico, where I had taken Harold Circuit's house for the winter of 1938 as a part of a general scheme of living, which was to hole up to write in odd but pleasant out-of-the-way places, and incidentally familiarize myself with new and interesting backgrounds and countries. For this is the most wonderful part of free-lance writing (when the world is at peace); your office is under your hat and you can live yourself into a place in short order and begin to work…readers of this series have frequently claimed that Hiram Holliday is autobiographical and that Hiram is myself. He is not myself at all, he is my alter ego. He is what I would like to see when I look into a mirror. And he certainly is what once I would have liked to have been."

'Crisis in London' gives us plenty of Hiram's backstory, "for fifteen years Holliday sat on the rim of the *Sentinel* copy-desk, correcting copy, writing headlines and checking up the work of men of action" until he saved his publisher from a $500,000 libel suit by virtue of the placement of a comma. That grateful publisher awarded him a bonus of $1,000 and a month's paid leave. Hiram decided to take a trip to Europe.

Hiram arrives in London on the *Britannique* and having experienced the city—a city on the brink of war—he heads for the *Sentinel*'s London office. There, for the first time in his life, he commandeers a typewriter and starts writing, "There will be no war, because England is England no more…London is blackmailed, naked and afraid…England has lost its strength, its wit and its guts…". He wrote and wrote, flung it on the Bureau Manager's desk and walked out. He goes for a walk but in Green Park he sees a woman and child being attacked. Hiram and his umbrella come to their rescue. Once they have escaped, and before the police arrive, the woman, who we learn is called Heidi, explains to Hiram that they are from Austria and that this was a kidnap attempt on Peter the young boy. Hiram helps them escape to Plymouth where they can catch the SS Bordeaux, which is bound for France. He then catches a train back to London. Reading some magazines on the way he discovers that he's been helping Princess Adelheit Von Furstenhof of Styria—known as Princess Heidi—and her nephew Duke Peter. Back in his room there's a couple of cablegrams waiting for him; one is from Joel Smith at the *Sentinel* telling him he's fired, the other is from Beuheld, the Managing Editor at the paper telling him he made Smith fire him, so that he could hire him—as a writer!

'Sanctuary in Paris', which appeared in the April edition of the magazine, adds some more details to Hiram's story; we discover he is five feet ten inches tall and was born in New York on August 10th, 1899. Beauheld sends Hiram to Paris, instructing Clegg, the bureau chief, to make use of him there. But Clegg doesn't know what to do with him. Somewhat melancholy after his adventure in London, Hiram buys a ticket to the Cirque Antoine. During the intermission of the performance he make the acquaintance of Lisette, one of the horse riders in the circus and he takes her to supper after the show. The following day he goes to a pipe shop to get his repaired but whilst there accidentally picks up and leaves with someone else's umbrella. He examines the umbrella and discovers a secret compartment with papers in. Those papers are mostly in Russian and given that a Russian General had recently disappeared and an undersecretary killed, Hiram tries to get the papers translated.

In the end he mails them to Beauheld at the Sentinel but when he returns to his hotel room, he's met by the man from the pipe shop looking to return his umbrella. A fight ensures, with the man producing a gun, but Hiram, with the help of his ju-jitsu, prevails, however he uses the wrong hold and his assailant is killed. Hiram flees, and seeing a group of men in the lobby waiting, he fears the worst and makes his way to his only friend in the city, Lisette. She is in her dressing room and Hiram manages to get dressed up as a clown before his pursuers start knocking. Hiram performs as Grognolle the clown and soon the show is a big hit. Soon though the *Sentinel* breaks the story using the papers Hiram sent them and Paris is even less safe for Hiram. Disguised as Grognolle, he makes his way to the airport and flies to Prague.

Which, unsurprisingly enough, is where 'Illusion in Prague', which was published in the May 1939 edition of *Cosmopolitan*, starts. Hiram has been looking for the Princess, who was thought to be living in exile in Prague, but with no success he returns dejectedly to his hotel. Somewhat cautious after his Paris adventure, in the lobby he spots a man with an obviously false beard but is distracted when he receives a cable from Beauheld which confirms they are squaring away the situation he left behind in Paris. Hiram meets up with Reck, the *Sentinel*'s local correspondent who invites him to a local party that would be filled with all sorts of high level people but Hiram is tired and plans to turn in, leaving Reck to go to the party alone. Getting some fresh air

Hiram spots the man with the false beard leaving the hotel and suspicious, he follows him…to the party that Reck is attending. Hiram discovers, much to his delight, that the host of the party is Princess Heidi.

Heidi introduces Hiram to her fiancé, Count d'Aquila. They, along with some friends, go to see Madam Ovenecka, who lives upstairs in the same apartment block. Also at the party is Madame Strakova, a high ranking government official and Hiram spots the man with the false beard making a beeline for her. Hiram finally gets to talk to Heidi and discovers that Peter is asleep in another room, and that they are both still wanted by the Nazis. But when Heidi takes Hiram to go and see Peter, the boy has disappeared. As they search the apartment Hiram makes his way outside in time to see the man with the false beard leaving in a cab. No one is able to find Peter and Hiram makes his way back to the hotel where, in the lobby, he sees the man with the false beard. Putting two and two together he tries to pull the beard off…only to discover it's real and that the man is a local dentist. He tries some more maths and realising who has kidnapped Peter, makes his way back to Heidi and they make their way to the apartment upstairs. There they discover Peter however a fight ensues and the kidnappers manage to get away with Peter. Hiram promises Heidi that he will find him.

'Death Notice in Berlin', which appeared in the July edition, starts rather ominously for our hero. On a November morning in Berlin a heavily bandaged Herman Weide is in court, charged with being a communist, working against the Third Reich and planning to set up an illicit broadcasting station. Weide maintains he is the victim of a plot and that his real name is Hiram Holliday; regardless, he is sentenced to be executed in a couple of days.

How did he get in this mess? He was sent to Berlin by Beauhold to cover the shooting of an Embassy secretary by a Jew. When the secretary dies the Sentinel's man in Berlin advises him to keep off the streets for his own safety. But Hiram is never one to do as he is told, so goes out for drinks and dinner. He comes across an antique store run by a Jew that is being attacked. The proprietor is attacked and beaten by storm troopers. Hiram spies a red-headed woman in a sports car watching the riot, but he can stand by no longer and attacks one of the storm troopers. But the storm trooper's colleagues start beating up Hiram and he is rescued by the red head who drives them to safety. She is the Grain Irmgarde von Helm, the partner of Dr Grunze, the evil Minister of Foreign Propaganda. At Irmgarde's mansion she and Hiram get to know each other—the morning after Hiram returns to his hotel and writes his story for the paper. But Irmgarde calls him and he returns to the mansion only to meet Dr Grunze. Hiram interviews Grunze and when the job is done, leaves to write up his interview. But he is mugged on the way back to the hotel and all his papers are stolen. He gets back to his room but hasn't been there long before he is visited by the police and the SS who accuse him of being Herman Weide, communist and they arrest him for high treason but not before they beat him badly.

In prison a heavily bandaged Hiram is visited by Irmgarde, who tells him how he has been set up by Grunze. Irmgarde has a plan to get him out; they swap clothes and she takes his place—assuring him that as the Grafin she won't be executed. She tells him to go back to her place and gather his things and flee to Paris. But she also tells him to avoid one room in the house.

Hiram does as he's told but too late, he realises what Irmgarde has done. She killed Grunze and this is her way of paying for her crime...

'Flight from Vienna' which was published in the August 1939 edition, sees Hiram having spent three months in Vienna having found no trace of Peter or Heidi. He goes for a drink with his friend Baron Willi von Salvator to Franzl's to hear Mitzi sing. In the bar some brown shirts come in and persecute one of the patrons, but the Baron stands up to them. As Mitzi starts to sing her attention is taken by a fat man, a woman and a little boy who are in the bar. She stops singing and disappears backstage – Hiram notices this, and he recognises the fat man and the boy as well. He formulates a quick plan with the Baron's help. Mitzi gets into their car and Hiram snatches the boy from the fat man. Amidst a hail of gunfire they make a quick getaway in their car.

The boy is Peter and Mitzi, Heidi. They head to the Wurstl Prater—amusement park—for as Hiram says, no one will think of looking for them there. But after a couple of rides they head for the shooting gallery but they are attacked by three men. They manage to escape into a taxi and seek sanctuary for a few days in a monastery. However they know they can't stay too long so make their escape and head for the border, however to do that they have to cross the Alps and eventually a shattered Hiram fears that they have failed, only to discover that they have in fact made it into Italy.

'Duello in Rome' which appeared in the September 1939 edition is the last of Hiram's adventures for now. Hiram had collapsed on the Italian side of the Alps unconscious and when he woke up Heidi and Peter were gone. The locals, understanding their situation, had passed them on from house to house whilst Hiram recovered. However when he was well enough the *Sentinel* sent Hiram to Rome where he again meets with Heidi and Peter who are being looked after by the Italians. However, Hiram's reputation has preceded him and he is soon being met by Lieutenant DI Cavazzo, a member of the Secret Council. Hiram has offended the Italian government with his articles about his adventures and Commendatore Ara-Pesca challenges Hiram to a duel. If he refuses, he'll be expelled from the country and portrayed in the Italian press as a coward. He accepts the challenge and writes what may be his last story for the paper. Coutn d'Aquila is also in Rome and Hiram asks him to help. As Hiram's the one who has been challenged, he can choose the weapons and he chooses a Roman sword. After a momentous battle Hiram wins the duel; however, he is seriously injured and it is two months before he can sail back to America. However, on the boat to New York he meets Heidi and Peter who are also going home...

The book itself was published in October by Alfred A Knopf and proved remarkably popular with a second edition going to print just a month later. Aside from the magazine serialisation many of the stories were also serialised in a variety of newspapers around the world and although the stories themselves are quite short, they were abridged for serialisation. Witness this, the opening paragraph to the book version of "Flight from Vienna":

> "It was the Baron who suggested that Sunday afternoon later in March, Hiram Holliday's last day in Vienna, that in the line of a farewell party they go to Franzl's in Grinzing to hear Mitzi sing Gassenhauer, old Viennese folk songs, later go on to the Cibenzl Terrace, overlooking all Vienna, for dinner, and perhaps wind up the evening with one of their absurd whirls through the "Wurstl Prater', the famous old amusement park. Hiram didn't care. He was leaving Vienna for Rome the next morning and was gloomy and depressed with a sense of failure, and yet in a way glad to be going."

Or this opening from *The Daily Courier*, July 18th, 1939:

"It was Baron Willi von Salvator who took Hiram Holliday, foreign correspondent, out to Franzl's Inn to hear Mitzi, the new toast of a chastened Vienna, sing old Viennese folk songs. Willi wanted to cheer Hiram up, for Hiram was in the doldrums. Hiram had promised himself that he would recover little Duke Peter of Styria who had been kidnapped by Virslany, the Nazi, in Prague, because he was a Hapsburg prince, and restore him to his sister Heidi, sweet princess Adelheit von Furstenhoff, with whom Hiram Holliday happened to be quite hopelessly in love. More than that, he had promised Heidi that he would find Duke Peter."

Reviews around the world were good; Australian papers, in a column entitled "What London is Reading" noted that "there is an added interest in this racy story in the fact that its author is an American, and that we consequently have American comments—expressed or otherwise—on the European scene during this last fateful year. Altogether this is a book in which thrills abound on a topical stage and invention rules; but since it is also a book in which the hero is a man of passionate ideals, and a hatred for evil tyranny, it is an interesting aside on current events."[1]

The Scotsman also liked the book:

"Mr Gallico is a new writer of romantic fiction, and his Hiram Holliday is the eternal crusader in modern guise. Hiram's almost incredible adventures are described with magnificent verve and fine skill. The reader finds himself intensely concerned with the outcome of a one-man crusade against the disintegrating forces of international gangsterism, and beset with anxiety lest the right should not prevail."[2]

A selection of other reviews from the time:

"Hiram is a queer card who drifts with extraordinary ease into the excitements of international crisis. In time, the thrill of his adventures gets somewhat blunted and interest in his oddity of character diminishes."[3]

"Mr Gallico's book is a brilliant and light-hearted piece of genuine entertainment with sufficient truth behind it to make it credible, at least at the time of reading…A genuine change this, from the ordinary crime or spy story."[4]

1 Cairns Post, 30th December, 1939
2 4th December 1939
3 Liverpool Daily Post, 3rd January 1940
4 Western Mail and South Wales News, December 14, 1939

Who Is Hiram Holliday?

"It is a story unique among thrillers and utterly enjoyable."[5]

"An exhilarating kaleidoscope of Europe on the eve of War."[6]

Such a popular book was bound to generate a sequel and just over a year after he made his first appearance in *Cosmopolitan*, Hiram was back in its pages. 'The Strange War of Hiram Holliday' was serialised from June to November 1940 and published under the title of *The Secret Front* in book form that autumn.

It was marketed as the continuing adventures of Hiram Holliday—which begs the question as to why he doesn't feature in the title—and indeed a plot summary suggests it is just more of the same; witness this from *The Cincinnati Enquirer* of 19 October 1940:

"In this second book Hiram carries on. In Warsaw he starts covering the German invasion for his paper. On an information seeking trip that takes him behind the German lines he observes the assassination of a German general and finds a stray paper from the General's notebook with a list of names. As Hiram proceeds on his adventurous way by air, truck, and submarine he discovers a pattern to which his list of names is a clue. Before the tale ends Hiram has saved a charming girl from destruction and laid bare the ramifications of a far-reaching Nazi plot."

Again the reviews were favourable:

"This book is swift, current, clear, and light as a feather. Straight out of the headlines of the early days of the war, Paul Gallico has assembled these further adventures of Hiram Holliday, his newspaper copyreader who burst through his green eyeshade to emerge as a johnny-on-the-spot at all the exciting moments. The photographers have a word for it. It is montage. You can see the author starting out with a handful of clippings about the sinking of the Athenia, the torpedoing of the Royal Oak at Scapa Flow, the Hon. Unity Freeman-Mitford, and the premature death of General von Fritsch. Mounting them side by side, Mr. Gallico has sketched in a connecting thread of plot and personal narrow escapes and somehow the thing hangs together. It is, in fact, a story. The names and incidents although sprayed with a thin coat of protective coloration are pleasantly recognizable and demonstrate effectively that truth is stranger than fiction. After a static thirty-page wind up the story shifts

---

5 The Birmingham Gazette, 3 Jan 1940
6 The Liverpool Echo, 20 December 1939

into blitz speed and rolls along with-out let or hindrance to an amiable finish. If only the season were summer, it would make perfect hammock reading."[7]

But there's something different about this book; whereas the first book was a collection of short stories this one is serialised novel and the pacing is different. There's more observations about the war, and the people involved in the war which make it fascinating to read eighty years after publication, but at the time it didn't offer the level of escapism that Hiram's audience wanted.

Gallico moved on, writing *The Snow Goose*, which was published in late 1940 in *The Saturday Evening Post* and in April 1941 in book form. But people were still asking him to bring back Hiram Holliday so he did, promising Frances Whiting, the Editor-in-Chief of *Cosmopolitan*, a further six adventures which would appear under the umbrella title of 'The Return of Hiram Holliday'.

The first, 'Terror Leaves Port Sheridan' appeared in the August 1942 edition and garnered a favourable reception with some critics calling it "a high spot in adventure stories"[8]. It was followed by 'The Enchanted Forest' in the September issue and 'Mission to Mexico' in the December edition. But, as Gallico would later explain, "the public, *Cosmopolitan*, and I all got tired of Hiram Holliday simultaneously and by mutual consent of Frances Whiting and myself the series and Hiram Holliday ended then and there. We just stopped the series without further ado, amidst no complaints whatsoever from the readers."[9]

With the benefit of hindsight he went on to analyse why Hiram's adventures had come to an end:

"We were in the war and Hiram had become an anachronism. In the first place, romance and adventure fiction simply has no place during a war, and anyone who tries to write it at that time is crazy. For super-romantic fact replaces fiction. Our Army, Navy, Marine, and Coast Guard kids, foot soldiers, fliers, O.S.S. men, commandos, and paratroopers were already performing in reality much more fabulous and thrilling deeds than could be dreamed up by any fiction writer. Against that background Hiram began to look pallid.

Secondly, if Hiram was such a heller, like Superman, why didn't he get into either the Army or the Navy and do something? But the Army didn't want a fat and

---

[7] Saturday Review of Books, 21st December 1940
[8] Shamokin News-Despatch, 8th July 1942
[9] Confessions of a Story Writer, 1947

bespectacled man over forty, just as they didn't want me, a tall, bespectacled oldster of forty-five. There was no place for either of us. I felt this keenly and it came out in the stories; it was immediately obvious that these stories were labored, forced, and lacking in the swing and zest and spirit of the early ones. Everything and everyone had changed.

The last I saw of Hiram he was down in Mexico City somewhere, having killed some Spanish Falangist, a Nazi agent, in a pistol duel. For all I know, he is there yet, a superannuated, outdated swashbuckler hanging out in the bar of the Reforms Hotel, mingling with the crowd of refugees, rich bums and draft-dodgers-afraid-to-come-home, drinking his pisco punches and lamenting the old days when a gentleman adventurer could go roman ticking about Europe and get some results. Time had done some marching on."

Gallico went on to write a total of forty-one books and numerous short stories throughout his life with many of them providing inspiration for film and TV productions. *The Snow Goose* had sealed his reputation as a storyteller with mass appeal "We live in a rough, cold world today," he once said. "But I make a different world when I write: I make it what I think it ought to be".

His 1958 novel *Mrs 'Arris Goes to Paris* was a best seller and became the first of a series of four novels about the lovable charwoman (which were eventually filmed with Angela Lansbury in the title role). His 1969 novel *The Poseidon Adventure* provided a template for many 1970s disaster movies and he was halfway through a sequel to the story when he died, in July 1976, at the age of seventy-eight in Monte Carlo. With an odd hint of Hiram, for the last few years of his life one of his chief forms of relaxation was fencing and he was fencing master to the French Army for many years until 1975.

Chapter Two: The Early Adventures of Hiram Holliday

Time had only marched on a little way when January 1945 brought a hint of things to come.

Gallico had established himself as a fiction writer—*The Snow Goose* had won the O Henry Award for short stories in 1941—and although he'd dabbled back in sports with his 1942 book on the baseball player Lou Gehrig, he was keen to move forward.

One of those ways, he thought, might be on radio. It was the pre-eminent medium for family entertainment throughout the 1940s and with the end of World War II the golden age of radio drama was really under way. Several of his stories had already been adapted for radio and he himself had been known to appear on shows such as *Information Please* – as part of the panel of experts that would attempt to answer questions submitted by listeners.

That month *Variety* reported that a half hour radio show based on *The Adventures of Hiram Holliday* was being "whipped into shape" and currently looking for a sponsor. Gallico himself was supervising the production and it was to be directed by New Yorker Ed Sanford who would produce alongside his partner Bill Richman. The script was by Lawrence Menken. Hindsight makes it interesting to note that Menken, who by then had already done a number of adaptations for radio, would go on to have a long career writing for radio, TV and occasionally in film. Richman and Sanford also went on to have long careers, but in music radio, well away from drama. Which might go some way to explaining as to why this iteration of Hiram's adventures never made it to air.

A few months later though, one of Hiram's adventures did indeed make it on air.

Curtain Time was an anthology show and like others at the time—such as *The First Nighter*—tried to emulate a theatrical experience for the listener by inviting them "to attend the evening's performance". It started on WMAQ in Chicago in 1935 before airing nationally on the Don Lee network in 1938 and would run until 1950 across a variety of networks. Several of Gallico's non-Hiram stories would be adapted for that version of the show. There was also a Canadian version, which was broadcast on CBC and it was they who got Hiram on air first. They produced a thirty-minute show called 'Adventure in Berlin' – an adaptation of Gallico's 'Death Notice in Berlin'—which aired at 9.30pm on Wednesday 25th April 1945.

Hiram was played by Canadian actor John Drainie, whom Orson Welles once termed 'the greatest radio actor in the world'. Born in Vancouver in 1916 Drainie was drawn to acting as a teenager, especially after a streetcar accident at 14 shattered his right hip and limited his physical pursuits. He started his career on stage where he always played older characters and became renowned for his ability to develop character from the inside out so that he could "become a character after immersing himself in the details of that character's life". He remained busy in Canadian radio but also made a successful move to television with guest shots in shows such as *The Alcoa Hour* (1956), *On Camera* (1955-58), and *Festival* (1961-95). His death from cancer at the age of fifty in 1966 cut short what could have been a long and well-regarded career.

He was just twenty-nine years old when he was cast as Hiram and had been working as an actor since before the war, when he was one of a number of performers who made it big in Vancouver and then moved to Toronto. Vivienne Herman starred as Grafin Irmgarde—Hiram's ambiguous German rescuer—and Lister Sinclair starred as a Nazi official. Amongst was the supporting cast of Tommy Tweed and Karen Glahn was Bernard Braden whose career as an actor and comedian would take off when he moved to the UK at the end of the 1940s. He did a number of comedy shows for BBC Radio before making a popular consumer affairs programme, *On the Braden Beat*, which aired on ITV for five years in the 1960s.

Hiram also nearly made his film debut that year as well, for MGM made an approach for the film rights for Spencer Tracy, who was keen to take on the starring role. But, as the press at the time reported, they weren't "able to buy the stories for him", possibly because someone else had an option on them already.

Five years later Hiram made his first TV appearance.

Although for many it seems to have been around forever, television is still a young industry. The first regularly scheduled service in the USA began in July 1928—though that was a 48-line system from an experimental station in Wheaton, Maryland. By 1939 NBC were offering regularly scheduled broadcasts in New York which they christened with the opening of the World's Fair. With the adoption of the NTSC standard in 1941 the FCC started issuing commercial licences in New York and Philadelphia.

World War II unsurprisingly halted development of any commercial service but it resumed after the end of the hostilities and just a few short years later the FCC was forced to stop issuing licenses due to high demand and concern that all these TV stations would interfere with each other. By early 1950 many of those issues had been resolved and the FCC started issuing licenses aplenty. And those licensees needed programmes to show.

A thirty-minute adaptation of 'Sanctuary in Paris' aired on 14th April 1950 as part of a weekly show called *The Play's the Thing*. This was an anthology show that was produced live by the Actor's Studio and presented adaptations of both original and classic dramas. The series had originated on ABC but by the time they got round to Hiram it had moved to CBS and had grown from 30 minutes to an hour in duration.

It was hosted by Marc Connelly, a Pulitzer prize-winning playwright and one of the wittiest members of the Algonquin Round Table. Forty-two-year-old Texan Elliott Sullivan was cast as Hiram. Sullivan was one of those actors who worked hard throughout his career but never really shone through, notching up almost a hundred films to his name but mainly in uncredited roles. He started his career aged just 22 in 1929 when he debuted on Broadway and established himself on stage before moving into film. Just a few years after playing Hiram he was called before the House Un-American Activities Committee in 1955 on the basis of testimony from more co-operative witnesses that stated he had been present at communist meetings. He refused to answer their questions invoking the First Amendment guaranteeing freedoms of speech and association and was indicted by a Federal grand jury in 1957 but acquitted by a Federal judge four years later because of a technicality—the prosecution failed to include in the indictment the resolution ordering the committee hearings. He moved to London in 1963 where he got roles in shows such as *The Persuaders* and *Public Eye*. He died from a heart attack in June 1974 on a visit to Los Angeles, aged just 66 years old.

Actress Joan Chandler made her TV debut playing Lisette, whilst other cast members included Richard Boone, who over a decade later would hit the big time starring as Paladin in *Have Gun – Will Travel*, Edward Kogan, Joseph A Kramm, Richard Malik, Reinhold Schunzel and a Canadian actor by the name of James Doohan. He, of course, is now best remembered for his role as Mr Scott on the original *Star Trek*. This small part was one of fifty-five live broadcasts he did from New York before moving to Toronto when his career started gathering speed.

Make-up on the show was done by Bob Jiras and publicity noted that "Jiras performed a bit of sleight of hand when, during "Sanctuary in Paris" on CBS-TV's "The Play's the Thing", actor Elliott Sullivan vanished into a dressing room—the cops chasing him—and came out 90 seconds later made-up and dressed as a clown. Greasepaint usually applied to a clown's face couldn't be used. It wouldn't go on fast enough. Instead, Jiras smeared on white pancake make-up with a sponge, dark pancake make-up on the lips (in place of lipstick) and slapped on a painted rubber nose (in place of nose putty). Two minutes later it all had to come off."[10]

Hiram was back on TV just over a year later in an adaptation shown as part of the *Philco Television Playhouse*. That show, a highly regarded anthology series, was broadcast live on NBC from 1948 to 1955. It was sponsored—unsurprisingly—by Philco, one of the pioneer manufacturers of radio and television sets.

'The Adventures of Hiram Holliday' was initially scheduled for Sunday February 25th that year but for reasons unknown, they aired an adaptation of a Max Wilk story, 'The Man Who Bought a Town' instead (which, in an odd coincidence, starred Elliott Sullivan). At the time some newspapers—still expecting Hiram to be on TV--noted that "If Hiram Holliday is played properly cast and directed, you will live with Hiram in a series of adventures on his trip to Europe, that you will long remember."[11]

Hiram eventually made it to air on Sunday 3rd June 1951.

"The Adventures of Hiram Holliday, a lively drama, will be presented on Philco Television Playhouse Sunday at 9. Hiram Holliday is a meek looking copyreader on a New York newspaper. However, he has unexpected sides to his character; he studies fencing, judo, boxing and marksmanship. When he received a reward from

---

10 Republican and Herald, November 12th, 1951
11 The Hartford Courant, 25th February 1951

his publisher for a job well done he decides to visit Europe and thence begin his adventures. He foils a plot by the Iron Curtain boys to kidnap a King and his daughter who are in Paris under assumed names trying to escape to America. He helps them to reach Spain and there the mad adventure reaches a spine-tingling climax when one of the King's trusted servants turns out to be an undercover worker for the spies. Hiram Holliday steps into the breach in a typical American manner to bring to television one of the most delightful heroes since Robin Hood."[12]

Hiram was played by an American actor, 37-year-old EG Marshall. He was an articulate, witty man with intense eyes and sharp features who is now probably best remembered for starring in the landmark 1960s legal drama *The Defenders* which became one of the defining role of his career as did that of neurosurgeon Dr David Craig in the 1969-73 show *The Bold Ones: The New Doctors*. On radio he is best remembered for serving as host of well-regarded anthology series *The CBS Radio Mystery Theater* from 1974 to 1982. He was often typecast as straitlaced and business-like characters—in *Superman II* he played the President and in *War and Remembrance* (1988-89) he played Dwight D Eisenhower. He kept busy throughout the 1980s with guest roles in shows such as *Murder She Wrote*, *The Equalizer* and *Spenser: For Hire*. He died from lung cancer in August 1998.

He had become interested in acting at a very young age and later recalled that he "used to watch movies—silent movies—and stock companies and theatre whenever I could". He would also perform wherever he could, be it school, church, the YMCA and community theatre. He made his Broadway debut in 1938 and relished working in theater. He also praised early television for taking chances, a strategy he thought abandoned as the medium got older. Often typecast as being straitlaced and business-like he was in many ways the ideal person to play an everyman hero such as Hiram Holliday.

Also in the cast were British actress Stella Andrew, Henry Calvin, Miriam Goldina, Adia Kuznetzoff and Ivan F Simpson.

The script was adapted by Alexander Kirkland, directed by Delbert Mann and produced by Fred Coe for Showcase Productions.

Reviews were not favourable with *Billboard*[13], in their own inimitable way, detailing the problems:

---

12 Courier Post, Saturday June 2nd, 1951
13 16th June 1951

"Paul Gallico's Hiram Holliday was an entertaining, escapist fiction about a newspaper drab who got hold of some scratch and had himself a time touring the world and running into semi-Graustarkian adventures. It was enjoyable reading but you'd never know it from the incredible mangling it got at the hands of Philco Playhouse. Part of the trouble seemed to stem from Alexander Kirkland's most unconvincing adaptation; part from Delbert Mann's rather flat direction.

There were times when the show verged on the ludicrous. There was a fight, for example, in which Holliday (played by EG Marshall) is supposed to rout a handful of Commie heavies, outduelling them with his umbrella. It just looked silly. In another incident, heavy no. 1, now hip to the fact that Holliday is hip to him, is supposed to knock him off by tying him to the target he uses in his chorus sharpshooting act. Only when the rescuers (natch) step in to untie him, the ropes fall off before they touch 'em. It was that kind of production.

Although Marshall, Stella Andrews and Miriam Goldina are first-rate actors, they were too handicapped by the sloppy production to breathe any life into the proceedings. Miss Andrews, however, is one of the more beautiful video ingenues with a delicate and classic appeal. Adia Kouznetzoff, more familiar for his singing in New York niteries, gave no life whatsoever to the deep dyed dastard.

In those early days of American television there was a fourth network that operated alongside ABC, CBS and NBC for a while. The DuMont Television Network operated from 1946 to 1956, having been established by DuMont Laboratories, one of the pioneers and developers of early television receivers, making them easily accessible for people at home. So a move into broadcasting seemed like a natural progression, although DuMont soon discovered they were at a disadvantage in not having the revenue from established radio broadcasting that supported NBC and CBS.

In 1951 they also realised they had a problem with their schedule; they had no hour long plays on it and shows such as the *Philco Television Playhouse* had shown that people liked to watch hour long plays. So they commissioned a show, *Cosmopolitan*

Theatre, an anthology series based on stories that originated in *Cosmopolitan Magazine*. It ran for just one season, airing in the last quarter of 1951.

Their first episode was a production of Gallico's second Hiram Holliday book *The Secret Front*, adapted by Richard Macaulay, produced and directed by Sherman Marks and aired live on Tuesday 2nd October. The cast included Marsha Hunt, Kurt Katch and Lee Tracy as Hiram.

Fifty-three years old at the time Tracy was by far the oldest actor to play Hiram. Born in Atlanta, Georgia in 1898 he grew up in Pennsylvania. He attended a military academy and served in World War I. After the War he became a US Treasury agent but within a couple of years the call of the stage was too strong and he returned to acting. He made his Broadway debut in 1924 and by 1929 was under contract to Fox Studios, making his film debut that same year. Several films followed but within a few years Tracey's fondness for nightlife and his perpetual absences from set gave him a well-deserved reputation as something of a troublemaker.

MGM offered him a contract in 1933 but in November that year, during the filming of the film *Viva Villa!* in Mexico City, he got into serious trouble. During a massive parade to celebrate the revolution against dictator Porfiro Diaz, Tracy stood on his hotel balcony clad only in a blanket shouting insults. The blanket reportedly slipped off. According to actor and producer Desi Arnaz, Tracy then urinated on the passing parade however other people, there at the time, dispute this. The fact remains that Tracy was charged with violating public morals and insulting the government and gave rise to such marvellous headlines such as "Lee Tracy Talks a Bit Too Loud".[14]

MGM chief Louis B Mayer described Tracy's behaviour as deplorable and after his contract with the studio had run its course Tracy freelanced, but the quality of his films declined. Although he periodically returned to the stage it was clear that TV seemed to be the best option for his talent. He starred as the Craig Rice character John J Malone in the 1951-52 series *The Amazing Mr Malone* and when that was cancelled after thirteen episodes moved almost immediately into a starring role as the eponymous private detective *Martin Kane*. But that didn't last long either—six episodes—and by the end of the 1950s he had a longer run as the star and narrator of the early ITC show *New York Confidential*. The starring roles petered out in the 1960s and he had to rely on a number of guest spots in shows such as *Wagon Train* and *Ben Casey*. In 1968 he was diagnosed with liver cancer and died in October that year, aged 70.

Marsha Hunt was also an interesting character. Born in Chicago in October 1917 her family moved to New York when she was young and she started performing in school plays and church functions. She graduated high school in 1934 but unable to find a college which would meet her requirements to study drama she found work modelling for the John Powers Agency and began taking acting classes. She was one

---

14 Wilmington Daily Press Journal, 21st November 1933

of the highest earning models in 1935 and planned to study stage acting at the Royal Academy of Dramatic Art in London.

However in June 1935, at the tender age of just 17, she signed a seven year contract with Paramount Pictures. Between 1935 and 1938 she made twelve pictures for them as well as two on loan to RKO and 20th Century Fox. However the studio terminated her contract in 1938 and she spent a few years starring in B movies for low budget studios, before signing a contract with MGM in 1941.

In 1947, disturbed by the actions of the House Un-American Activities Committee she and her husband, screenwriter Robert Presnell, Jr started actively campaigning against them. Ultimately, she was told that if she wanted to find more work in Hollywood she would have to denounce her activities. She refused. In 1950, along with 151 other actors, writers and directors, she was named as a potential Communist or a Communist sympathiser by the anti-Communist publication *Red Channels*. Work became scarce for her and her husband and during the next eight years, whilst blacklisted she made only a handful of films.

In 1957 her career picked up however she announced her semi-retirement in 1960. She made a few appearances in film and TV—including in an episode of *Star Trek: The Next Generation*—as well as writing a book and producing a CD of songs she had written. At the time of writing she lives in California, at the age of 101.

Reviews for the show were generally encouraging:

"The series opened with a TV adaptation of Paul Gallico's "The Secret Front", a story of six marked for death because they knew too much about a fake Hitler. Film shots were deftly blended with studio sequences to give the production scope and flexibility that cannot be achieved on stages alone."[15]

"*The Cosmopolitan Theater*, on the other hand, makes no attempt to crown itself with a halo of artistry. Its design is simply to offer an enjoyable show. And this is exactly what it did one night when it telecast Lee Tracey and Marsha Hunt in a thrilling adventure yarn by Paul Gallico, "Secret Front". It involved Gallico's famous character Hiram Holliday, the dashing foreign correspondent, a fellow made for TV."[16]

But for this incarnation of Hiram there were to be no further adventures.

---

15 The Chicago Tribune, 8th October 1951
16 Daily News, Saturday October 20th, 1951

Chapter Three: The Return of Hiram Holliday

Hiram's next, and most successful appearance on television was entirely down to one man: Philip Rapp.

Rapp was a writer, director and producer who was born in Hull, England on 26 March 1907 and moved to America with his family when he was just sixteen years old. They settled in New York, in the Bronx, and life fell "into the usual routine". But young Phil had aspirations and by the age of nineteen he was performing on stage in vaudeville. That experience put him in touch with a number of comedians who were so impressed with his quick wit that they started to pay him to write jokes for them.

In 1931 he started writing for radio on *The Chase & Sanborn Tea Program*, a fifteen minute twice weekly show that aired over CBS and starred vaudeville singer and comic Georgie Price. After writing for that and the sister show *The Chase & Sanborn Coffee Program* he went on air himself as the master of ceremonies of the interestingly named *The US Industrial Alcohol Program*, a fifteen minute program touting Pyro anti-freeze. But he returned to writing and soon found himself writing for the likes of Eddie Cantor—one of vaudeville's biggest stars—and George Burns. By 1935 he was working with David Freedman, writing *The Eddie Cantor Show* for Chase & Sanborn. The previous year they'd contributed a number of sketches to the *Ziegfeld Follies of 1934* stage show. One of those sketches introduced what turned out to be one of Rapp's most endearing creations, Baby Snooks, a mischievous young girl who was forty years younger than Fanny Brice, the actress who played her. Snooks became a regular on radio and in 1944 was given her own show, written by Rapp, which went on to become one of the country's most popular sit-coms.

Some of his sketches featured a married couple who spent a lot of their time in verbal warfare. He called them The Bickersons and by 1946 they had graduated to their own show, written by Rapp, which would run very successfully for several years on CBS. They tried to adapt it several times for TV in the early 1950s but none met with the success the radio version had. It was clear to Rapp that television was the way to go. (In some of the pre-publicity for *The Adventures of Hiram Holliday*, he would later suggest that he'd been trying to get Hiram on TV for almost ten years. That desire had undoubtedly been frustrated by the early TV adaptations which had rendered the rights unavailable.)

In 1953 he was hired to write and script edit the TV adaptation of the *Topper* books by Thorne Smith. He would go on to write twenty episodes of the half-hour show but more importantly it became a useful template for him, for as script editor and thus working closely with the producers, he got a good understanding of how to put together a thirty minute comedy.

Indeed it was *Topper*'s producer Bernard Schubert who got Rapp launched on his next production. In November 1955, with *Topper* cancelled, he sent Rapp a telegram: "CAN GET TV HIRAM HOLLIDAY. HOW MUCH MONEY DO YOU WANT TO GO WITH ME FOR SIX MONTHS". Which, translating from the telegramese, meant that Schubert could get a six-month option on the TV rights to Hiram Holliday. He had approached the MCA Agency, who represented Paul Gallico and they indicated a deal might be possible.

But a couple of days after sending that telegram Schubert talked with Bertha Case, Gallico's agent, who advised that other networks and show packagers were interested in the rights as well. It seemed like there was competition to get Hiram on TV but in the end Rapp, who managed to get NBC on board with his pitch won out, securing a six-month option on the TV rights for $750.

When the deal was done George Gruskin, his agent, sent Rapp a telegram: "DEAR PHIL. I HAVE SPENT ALL MORNING TRYING TO THINK UP APPROPRIATE FRENCH PHRASES FOR THIS WIRE, BUT I DON'T HAVE A FRENCH-ENGLISH DICTIONARY IN THIS RENTED HOUSE, SO THE BEST I CAN SAY IS "TOUJOURS LE RAPP, TOUJOURS LE TALENT, TOUJOURS LE SUCCESS." I DON'T KNOW WALLY BUT

PLEASE GIVE HIM THE SAME WARM WISHES FOR, AND BELIEF IN, THE SMASH HIT THAT YOU KNOW IS IN MY HEART FOR YOU. AFFECTIONATELY..."

'Wally' was Wally Cox, the only person Rapp ever envisaged playing Hiram and a well-known actor just coming off a high profile show.

Born Wallace Maynard Cox in Detroit, Michigan on December 6th, 1924 his early life was fairly nomadic, and he attended nine separate schools in twelve years. At the age of ten, along with his divorced mother, mystery writer Eleanor Blake, and his younger sister, he moved to Evanston, Illinois where he became close friends with another child in the neighbourhood, Marlon Brando. Eventually the Cox family settled in New York and in 1942 he enrolled in a botany course at the City College.

He joined the Army Enlisted Reserve and was called to active duty in March 1943. "The Army gave me the usual tests" Cox later told interviewers[17] "and found I had a high mechanical aptitude. So where did I wind up? In the infantry. I lasted four months. Five days a week I worked in a message center. On Saturdays the message center personnel had to go on all day hikes. I never finished a hike. So they put me in the hospital, examined me, and gave me a physical discharge."

For a time he worked on a Long Island farm then he got a job in a radio factory, underwent a spell in a hospital for treatment of "a nameless ailment, most likely chronic fatigue" and finally decided to be scientific about planning his future. He went to a guidance counsellor in New York, paid $20 and took a series of aptitude tests. "I scored two per cent in inductive reasoning and was told never to attempt anything creative or imaginative. They told me I should make things with my hands and play musical instruments, not the piano. I wanted to be a success in life so I followed instructions. Besides, I didn't want to waste the twenty bucks."

He enrolled at New York University under the GI Bill to study arts and crafts but left there when his mother became ill. He went to work for a silversmith, "a fellow who expressed deep sympathy for the working man while he paid me 86 cents an hour" but as you might imagine from that statement, he didn't stay long. He set up as a silversmith in his own right and made a living selling silver cufflinks to men's shops.

In the spring of 1944 he looked up Marlon Brando, who was still in the early stages of his career. Brando invited him to a number of theatrical parties and Cox discovered that people found his offhand comments about arts and crafts hilariously

---

17 This one from The Philadelphia Inquirer of November 30th, 1952

funny. A few years later Cox joined a small theatre group in Greenwich Village but it fell apart after a month however the director of the group, George Auerbach, suggested that Cox polish his monologues and audition for Max Gordon, owner of a nightclub called the Village Vanguard, which had a reputation for discovering new talent.

The audition was a success and for the next three years he made his living playing nightclubs. He also signed for a role in the short lived musical revue *Dance Me a Song* and promptly stole the show. His big opportunity came in late 1951 when he starred in a whimsical episode of the *Philco Television Playhouse* called 'The Copper'. Both David Swift, the writer of that show, and Fred Coe, the producer, knew they had a rare personality in their midst, someone who deserved a show of his own.

Swift created a show called *Mister Peepers*, which featured Cox as the eponymous character, a shy science teacher at Jefferson Junior High, who is always faced with problems but never outwitted. It was sponsored by Ford and aired, initially, as a summer fill-in show running from July to September 1952. But less than three weeks after it ended NBC received around fifteen thousand letters demanding more. It made Wally Cox a star.

The Reynolds Metals Co., which had been sponsoring the short-lived and forgettable sitcom *Doc Corkle*, took one look at the response to *Mister Peepers* and switched their advertising budget. Cox would go on to play Peepers for a hundred episodes between 1951 and 1955. In a quote given at the height of his fame as Mr Peepers he said "Except for my close friends most people have taken it for granted I'm naturally ridiculous. I thought about this a great deal and decided that since people tended to laugh at me, I'd turn the situation into gainful employment. Mr Peepers is an exaggeration of what folks think of me when I'm odd".[18]

The show was nominated for an Emmy in 1954 and Cox himself won a Peabody Award for the role but as often with these things after a few years it began to slip. The character had changed—he'd gotten married—with some critics deriding the show as another *I Love Lucy*.

When *Mister Peepers* went off-air in June 1955 Phil Rapp revisited his plans for Hiram and started negotiations with Cox. George Gruskin at the William Morris Agency, encouraged him to pursue the idea of getting Hiram on to television "because I thought the treatment of such a project in the hands of his unique talents would

---

[18] Arizona Republic, February 8th, 1953

result in an outstanding series"[19] But Cox wasn't an easy sell to the sponsor; John Brady, a General Foods executive, "didn't want to look at the pilot at all because he told me frankly half a dozen times that he literally hated Wally Cox as a performer," according to Gruskin. "'Finally, because of Rod's belief in my description of the show, and in my opinion of Rapp's tremendous talent and experience and the fact that this was a different Wally Cox than the public had ever seen, I was able to corner Brady with Rod's assistance. Brady and Erickson agreed to view the pilot at our office and to meet with Phil at the same time in order to discuss the scope and plans for the series beyond the pilot. I had had Phil prepare several dozen exciting story springboards.

When Brady saw the film and listened to Phil's presentation of future planning, he changed his attitude completely and before he and Rod left our screening room, they both said this was the best show they had seen for their purpose and the one they definitely wanted."

Phil loved Wally Cox, calling him "articulate, literate and athletic. He could handle any stunt. He was a tireless worker who knew his lines to perfection and needed very little direction but questioned almost everything. He learned to fence with the skill of a *master*."

So Rapp had the rights, he had a star, he had a network potentially on board... he needed a pilot script. Whilst he could have written it himself Rapp was firmly on board as the producer, the showrunner, to use 21st century parlance. Plus, he wanted to direct some of the episodes himself which meant his time was already at a premium.

He hired writer Richard M. Powell to write the pilot. Powell would go on to write a number of episodes for the show but had been blacklisted so always ceded credit for them to Rapp.

Powell was born in Cincinnati, Ohio on 15 December 1916. He attended the local university where he pursued a liberal arts degree and started writing. "I was a writer in the campus newspaper. I had my own column in which I gave everybody hell, which was a lot of fun. I wanted to be a newspaperman when I got out of college, but I couldn't get anybody to read my material."[20] His father had insisted he attend law school after graduation but it wasn't long before both of them realised that wasn't a good idea. He abandoned the law and got a job as a comedy writer for WLW radio in Cincinnati. When war broke out, he enlisted in the Army Entertainment Corps

---

19 Ben Ohmart book on Rapp
20 Shedding Light on the Hollywood Blacklist, Stanley Dyrector (Bearmanor, March 2013)

which would ultimately keep him in the USA for the duration of his four years' service. He rose to the rank of Captain.

After the War he returned to his job at WLW but "somebody did me a great favour and fired me, so I set my sails for California". That was in 1946 but again he struggled to get a break. Edgar Bergen, popular radio star who was known to give new writers a break, rejected his work as did several others. Eventually his break came from a show on the east coast which offered to buy his submission for $500. That got him an agent and the agent got him a job on the popular radio show *The Life of Riley*, He was there for two years before budget cuts meant he was eventually let go.

Other freelance radio work followed—including several episodes of *The Adventures of the Saint* and a long stint writing for Fred MacMurray and Irene Dunne—but the landscape was changing. It was the time of the anti-communist blacklist and a New York based publication, *Red Channels*, had published a book, about two inches thick, which detailed the name of every actor, writer and producer who had ever gone on a march or gone to a meeting. They were talking about putting out a Hollywood edition and at a mass public meeting Powell was one of the speakers against it. He found himself losing work because of speaking out and was soon blacklisted himself. In late 1952 he was nominated for and won the presidency of the newly formed Television Writers of America—a branch of the Writers Guild—"which is seeking to become bargaining agent for writers of Hollywood originating live and filmed TV shows." He served as president for many years during the subsequent decade and would remain active in the Guild for the rest of his life. Writer Sy Gomberg later recalled him as "…the most courageous guy I knew in the Guild and he truly believed in the Guild and promoting the well-being of the writers. Everyone, even those who didn't share his views, had tremendous respect for him and what he had to say."

That same year he was hired to work on *Topper* –"I worked under the name of the head writer on the show who understood my situation and was willing to put his name on it. Of course, the only difficulty with it was that I was getting half-scale but what could I do?" That writer? Phil Rapp.

In 1953 Powell married Libby Burke, a dancer who had refused to testify during the communist witch-hunt. Her daughter Jenifer remembers "…we used to call him affectionately Dickie. At first I was a bit intimidated by him because he was such a big man, maybe 6'3" and 200 pounds…but I soon learned he was indeed a very kind and thoughtful man…he loved to cook and remodelled parts of our home." Burke fell pregnant but tragically died in childbirth in 1956.

Dick was devasted but he eventually found love again with Alice Shragowitz, a psychotherapist original from Minneapolis. They married on New Year's Eve 1962 and had two children, Anthony and Alex. He contributed four episodes to both *The Gomer Pyle Show* and *The Andy Griffith Show*; they were well received and producer Ed Feldman hired him to rewrite the pilot episode of a show called *Hogan's Heroes*. Feldman liked his work so much that he didn't change a single word of the script and Dick went on to write four of the first five episodes and would ultimately write twenty-nine through the six-year run of the show.

After *Hogan's Heroes* he would contribute episodes to shows such as *M*A*S*H*, *Quincy* and *Charlie's Angels* before his death in October 1996, dying from cancer at the age of 79.

Phil Rapp wrote to Powell in early October 1956, clarifying their relationship:

"Dear Richard,

Since—because of nauseous circumstances which are at the present beyond the control of both of us—a formal contract between us on *The Adventures of Hiram Holliday* is not now possible, the following letter will serve to spell out our relationship on the show.

It is understood that your present price per script is to be $1,500 for the present season and if we are renewed for the 1957-58 season your price per script will be $2,000. In addition, any work done by you on scripts written by other writers will be compensated in each individual case at a price agreeable to both of us. Naturally I will want you to write as many scripts as it is humanly possible for you to do.

It will be further understood that on scripts where my name appears as the writer you are to receive any re-run payments due under the MBA schedule for such payments. (If in the future I actually write teleplays for Hiram Holliday such rerun payments will naturally go to me)

In addition to the above payments, 10% of my share of any and all profits on Hiram Holliday will be paid to you whenever profit payments are received by me.

This letter is intended for your protection, and copies will go to my accountant and to my wife, to be kept on file by them. I will of course not cease my efforts to get for you the credit you so richly deserve on Hiram Holliday and—since your present problem stems from attempts to obtain fair working conditions for all writers—I do not expect you to give up fighting because of the fact that injustice is now being visited upon you."

On June 9th, 1956, with all key players on board—Phil Rapp had signed on as a freelance director, earning $750 per film—the public announcement was made that "General Foods is to sponsor Adventures of Hiram Holliday starring Wally Cox on NBC-TV, starting October 3rd, through Young & Rubicam".[21] Ultimately General Foods would use the show to promote two of their brands; Sanka instant coffee and Jello.

The show was to be made through California National Productions (CNP) for NBC. CNP was a subsidiary of the network formerly known as Kagran Corp, which has started life solely focused on merchandising. But around the same time the Holliday series was announced NBC decided to combine merchandising together with a number of other activities all under the one corporate banner, bringing together television production, distribution, merchandising and other related activities. It united the California National Studios, NBC Television Films, the merchandising division and the NBC Theatrical Division, which administered the NBC Television Opera Theatre and the NBC touring opera company.

CNP rented four stages on the California Studios lot and maintained an option to lease the entire studio in the long term. The studios were at 5530 Melrose Avenue and it was there, on stage 4, that the pilot was shot at the end of March 1956. The series went into production on the same lot in July that year. One of the other stages rented by CNP was occupied by *The Life of Riley*, a TV adaptation of the radio show that Richard Powell had worked on, which had already been on air for a couple of years.

On 24 May 1956 the pilot was aired before a test audience in New York. In their report back to the producers the Research Department of Young & Rubicam noted that:

"Each juror recorded his opinion as the program proceeded by means of a General Electric Opinion Meter. These opinions were electrically averaged and graphed on a moving tape, the mid-point of which was set at 50. The Enjoyment Ratings and Program Profile were derived from this tape. This is the procedure for all programs tested.

---
21 Billboard and Television Digest both covered the story and used this line on that date.

In addition to the electrically recorded opinions, the jurors were asked questions at the completion of the program, to obtain more detailed information concerning their reaction to the program.

Enjoyment Rating

This presentation of Hiram Holliday received an over-all enjoyment rating of 63. The over-all comedy average is 63 and the overall audition average is 61. The over-all TV average for all programs tested to date is 59.

Portion of Program Liked Most

Forty-one per cent of the jurors mentioned liking the story in general terms, among those twenty per cent liked the humor of the show and ten per cent thought it was an entertaining show. Twenty-two per cent of the jurors mentioned liking some specific scenes. Eight per cent liked the fencing scenes and seven per cent liked the lion in the stateroom scene. Twenty per cent of the jurors mentioned liking Wally Cox. Sixteen per cent of the jurors said they liked everything about this show.

Portion of Program Liked Least

Twelve per cent of the jurors mentioned disliking the characters, among these five per cent disliked Wally Cox, and three per cent disliked the Englishman. Seventeen per cent of the jurors mentioned disliking the story in general terms. Three per cent thought it was inane, and three per cent did not like the canned laughter. Another three per cent stated that the Audience Jury laughed too loud. Thirty-eight per cent of the jurors said that there was nothing they disliked about this show.

Thermometer of Program

Eighty-six per cent of the jurors would like to see another presentation of Hiram Holliday. Sixty-nine per cent were very much in favour of seeing another show. Eight per cent of the jurors were very much against seeing another show.

Comparison of Enjoyment Ratings

This presentation of Hiram Holliday received an over-all enjoyment rating of 63. The over-all comedy average is 63 and the over-all audition average is 61. The over-all TV average for all programs tested to date is 59.

Programs	Over-All Enjoyment Ratings
Auditions	
Phil Silvers (Audience Jury: 16th Dec 1954)	61
People's Choice (Audience Jury 8th June 1955)	60
People's Choice (Audience Jury 9th June 1955)	64
Buckley (Audience Jury 27th April 1955)	62
Stanley (Audience Jury 8th February 1956)	58
Happy People (Audience Jury 2nd May 1956)	54
Regular Shows	
Those Whiting Girls (average of 3 shows)	62
Johnny Carson Show (average of 6 shows)	62
Our Miss Brooks (Average of 30 shows)	66
Ray Milland Show (Average of 5 shows)	65
Averages	
Over-all TV average	59
Over-all Audition Average	61
Over-all comedy average	63
Hiram Holliday	63

Question asked:
"What one thing did you like most about this show?"

Summary of Responses:

Forty-one per cent of the jurors mentioned liking the story in general terms, among these twenty per cent liked the humor of the show, and ten per cent thought it was an entertaining show. Twenty-two per cent of the jurors mentioned liking some specific scenes. Eight per cent liked the fencing scenes, and seven per cent liked the lion in the stateroom scene. Twenty per cent of the jurors mentioned liking Wally Cox. Sixteen per cent of the jurors said they liked everything about this show.

Responses	All Jurors (%)
Specific Scenes	
Fencing scenes	8
The lion in the stateroom	7
When he danced with the girl	5
When the Editor gave him the check	2
Characters and acting	
Wally Cox	20
The Lion	3
Good acting	3
General	
Humor, good comedy	20
Good story	3
Plot	3
Entertaining	3
Adventure	2
Idea of story	2
Courage of Hiram Holliday	2
Hiram Holliday's face	2
No interruptions	2
Script	2
Everything	16
Nothing	5
No report	5
Because of multiple mentions total adds up to 115.	

Portion of program liked least:

Question Asked
"What one thing did you like least about this show?"

Summary of Responses:
Twelve per cent of the jurors mentioned disliking the characters, among these five per cent disliked Wally Cox, and three per cent disliked the Englishman. Seventeen per cent of the jurors mentioned disliking the story in general terms. Three per cent thought it was inane, and three per cent did not like the canned laughter. Another three per cent stated that the Audience Jury laughed too loud.

Thirty-eight per cent of the jurors said there was nothing they disliked about this show.

Responses	All Jurors (%)
Specific scenes	
Scene with the girl	3
When he was drugged	2
Characters	
Wally Cox	5
Englishman	3
The Girl	2
The Lion	2
General	
Too inane	3
Audience Jury laughed too loud	3
Laughter on sound track	3
Girl's voice	2
Foreign element overdone	2
Hard to understand dialogue	2
Melodramatic acting	2
Everything	3
Nothing	38
No report	28
Because of multiple mentions total adds up to 103	

Thermometer of Program

Question asked:
"Please put a check opposite the statement that best indicates your enjoyment of the television program you have just viewed."

Summary of Responses:
Eighty-six per cent of the jurors would like to see another presentation of Hiram Holliday. Sixty-nine per cent were very much in favour of seeing another show. Eight per cent of the jurors were very much against seeing another show.

Responses	All Jurors (%)
I would very much like to see another presentation of Hiram Holliday	69
I would like somewhat to see another presentation of Hiram Holliday	17
I don't care whether I see another presentation of Hiram Holliday	3
I don't think I would like to see another presentation of Hiram Holliday	3
I would not at all like to see another presentation of Hiram Holliday	8

Suggestions for Improving Program:
Question asked: "What suggestions do you have for improving this program?"

Summary of Responses:
There were no suggestions recorded by a significant number of jurors. Less than ten per cent of all jurors is not considered to be significant.
More than half of the jurors said they had no suggestions to offer.

By August Joel Malcolm Rapp, Phil Rapp's eldest son, was hired as story editor for the show on a salary of $300 per week. Although he'd gotten a break courtesy of his father and written an episode of *Topper* ('The Package') he'd worked on shows such as *Highway Patrol* and *Science Fiction Theatre* before being professionally reunited with Rapp Senior. After working on the show Rapp Junior went on to write for numerous other shows including *McHale's Navy* and *Gilligan's Island* and subsequently established himself as a horticultural guru, setting up his own indoor plant business in Hollywood and writing several best-selling books on indoor gardening. He also spent eleven years as the TV gardener on *Regis and Kathy Lee*.

Cast as Hiram's comic foil, Joel Smith, was actor Ainslie Pryor. Thirty-five years old, he was born James Ainslie Pryor in Memphis, Texas and before going to Hollywood spent six years as the director and manager of a Little Theater group in Raleigh, North Carolina. In 1954 he played the role of the prosecutor in the original company of *Caine Mutiny Court Martial*, starring alongside Henry Fonda. It was written by Herman Wouk and ran on Broadway for a year. The following year he got his first credited TV role in the NBC show *Big Town* and that same year recreated his Caine Mutiny role for a TV adaptation on the show *Ford Star Jubilee*. A number of guest roles in a variety of shows ensued but *The Adventures of Hiram Holliday* was his first regular gig.

Sadly, it was also one of his last for he died of cerebral cancer on May 27th 1958 at the age of 37. He had been diagnosed the previous December but refused to remain in hospital and played five roles on TV post diagnosis. He was reportedly preparing for a role on *Playhouse 90* before entering hospital.

In a recurring role as Hiram and Joel's boss, Harrison Prentice, was veteran actor Thurston Hall. Hall, born in 1882 in Boston seemed to specialise in playing big, blustery authoritarian roles which the leading man or woman could play off. He was another graduate from *Topper*, where he'd played Leo G Carroll's bewildered, blustering boss, Mr Schuyler but he'd made his Broadway debut at the age of 22 in 1904 and his earned his first film credit in 1915. He had an ongoing role in the Lone Wolf film series as Inspector Crane and in the 1950 *Dick Tracy* TV series as Diet Smith but despite a long and successful career these, and his role as Mr Prentice were his only regular gigs. He died at the age of 75 in Los Angeles in February 1958.

Ainslie Pryor as Joel

Pre-publicity for the show crept into gear several weeks before the show's scheduled October 1956 debut. Phil Rapp explained Hiram's origins in a newspaper column published in August by the United Press agency.

Hiram and Marlene take several turns round the dance floor

I was sorry to see "Mr Peepers" go. He was a nice fellow and he was around so long I'd grown to like him.

But I can't lament his passing too greatly. For ten years I've wanted to put "Hiram Holliday" on film, and in my mind at least, there was only one person cut out to play the part—Wally Cox. When "Peepers" folded on NBC TV I saw my chance and started negotiations with Wally right away.

For one thing "Peepers" had a single dimension. He was the shy and somewhat bewildered schoolteacher whose response in any situation was predictable. "Hiram" preserves much of "Peepers" but adds something.

In the new TV series Hiram Holliday, a character created by Paul Gallico for Cosmopolitan Magazine in 1939, is an obscure proof-reader on a New York newspaper. His spare dollars and hours are devoted to developing an amazing knowledge of the world and physical skills like fencing, swimming, judo etc. so that beneath the innocuous façade of proof-reader he is really a highly trained athlete, sort of a pint-sized Douglas Fairbanks.

Hiram's adventures begin when, by catching a transposed comma, he saves the publisher from a million-dollar damage suit. The publisher sends him on a round the world trip and assigns a reporter to write about his adventures.

Thus, Wally gets to show an underside of his nature that could never burst out of the "Peepers" frame. For his first "Hiram Holliday" film he had to learn to fence. After three weeks at it the instructor said he was doing as well as students with six months practice.

In the second film Cox had to hang by an umbrella handle from the belt of a trapeze artist. All this while the trapeze was swinging 30 feet off the ground. In succeeding episodes, he fights on top of a moving train, performs intricate Spanish dances, boxes, rides a motorcycle and skin dives. Wally already is a skin diver and is as much at home in a motorcycle saddle as Peepers was behind a school desk. The other skills he'll learn as he goes along.

Hiram Holliday is another Walter Mitty, the difference being he can really do the thing Mitty dreams about. The result so closely approximates Wally's own life he's sometimes embarrassed by the comparison. The other day he told an admirer "If you'll permit me to stretch a point, I suppose you could say Hiram Holliday and Wally Cox are somewhat the same person."[22]

That closeness of character between Hiram Holliday and Wally Cox was something the show played on and undoubtedly helped with the publicity. But one executive from Young & Rubicam was concerned about this writing that "If one were to cast this role ideally, it would probably be with someone who is physically more robust and possibly better looking." But, they'd agreed before the series started that Wally was perfect for the role. "Since his physical equipment is certainly adequate, you may want to show more scenes with Wally indicating his actual strength in order to further the believability."

This is a compilation of the press releases they issued prior to the show's debut:

---

22 This came from the 23 August 1956 edition of *The Daily Notes* but it was carried in many papers.

The Life and Times of Hiram Holliday alias Wally Cox
Whoever Paul Gallico had in mind when he created "Hiram Holliday" for a *Cosmopolitan* magazine series in 1939, it was doubtless not one Wallace Maynard Cox, then a bespectacled youngster more concerned with outdoor life in his native Michigan than with footlights.

Without realizing it, however, Gallico carefully drew a picture of what Cox was to become—a shy, mild-mannered young man whose deceptively boyish face and figure belie an encyclopaedic mind and strong, supple muscles.

In a sense, Wally Cox, the former "Mr Peepers" of television, has been training all his life to become Hiram Holliday.

"I'm a little embarrassed by the verisimilitude of our lives," Wally admits frankly when a comparison is brought up. "I suppose if one were permitted to stretch a point, he would say that Hiram Holliday and Wally Cox are somewhat the same person."

Wally Cox buckled on his spiritual and physical armour, shined his spectacles to a high degree of visibility and sharpened the ferrule on his umbrella for combat in his latest television comedy series. Perhaps a word about the correct name-spelling of his Paul Gallico character is in order now.

It isn't Hirum Holiday.

Hiram Holiday neither.

Nor is it Hiram Halliday (although Gallico's original proof-reader turned knight in drab armour went under that moniker).

Nor is it spelled Holyday, Haliday, Holladay.

In short, Wally Cox's name in the series is again and for evermore Hiram Holliday.

WALLY COX RETURNS AS STAR IN "ADVENTURES OF HIRAM HOLLIDAY" ENACTING (SEEMINGLY) MEEK FELLOW WHO'S (REALLY) A WONDER MAN.

Wally Cox, who earned TV comedy fame on the "Mr Peepers" series, returns to television with his famous escapades in THE ADVENTURES OF HIRAM HOLLIDAY.

Based on the *Cosmopolitan* magazine stories by Paul Gallico, "The Adventures of Hiram Holliday" is a mixture of mirth and rousing melodrama. Wally plays the title role as an obscure proof-reader on a New York newspaper who devotes all his spare time and money to becoming expert at every known physical skill.

Pushed to action—as indeed he is quite often—Hiram proves himself capable of coping with the most taxing situations. He can best a master swordsman, surprise a champion wrestler with vise-like holds, subdue waterfront thugs with a few quick judo tricks, and even tame a snarling lion. He travels around the world with his trip paid for by a grateful publisher whom Hiram saved from a $1,000,000 libel suit by discovering a misplaced comma.

THIS MOPPET PREFERS HIRMA'S BUMBERSHOOT TO CROCKETT'S RIFLE

The Wally Cox comedy series, The Adventures of Hiram Holliday, back on television to delight the young and the young in heart.

One fan reports this backyard exchange: "You be Davy Crockett and I'll be Bat Masterson," one youngster shouted to another brandishing his grandfather's cane, "and see who wins"

But the second youngster didn't like the role cut out for him.

"I don't want to be Davy Crockett," he said pointedly. "Davy Crockett is old-fashioned, he shoots bears and there aren't any bears around here."

"Who do you want to be?"

"Hiram Holliday" the second youngster shouted without hesitation.

"But you can't be Hiram Holliday," retorted the first, waving his cane, "Where you goin' to get an umbrella?"

BEHIND HIRAM HOLLIDAY'S MEEK FAÇADE IS A MAN OF UNIQUE—IF COMIC—PROWESS

Wally Cox, television and nightclub comedian whose offbeat approach to conventional situations in his "Mr Peepers" show first won him national prominence, returns to TV in the hilarious series, *The Adventures of Hiram Holliday*.

As Hiram Holliday, a character created by Paul Gallico in a series of short stories written for Cosmopolitan Magazine, Cox is a disarmingly quiet newspaper proof-reader. Behind this façade of meekness, however, Cox has developed surprising skill in many of the physical arts. In a fencing duel, for example, Hiram Holliday can be counted on to come through against the master swordsman.

Hiram's publisher becomes so impressed with his proof-reader's physical prowess that he sends Hiram on a round-the-world trip. A reporter, played by actor Ainslee

Pryor is sent along to record Hiram's adventures on the trip. These accounts make up the series.

In the series "Hiram Holliday" is an obscure proof-reader on a New York newspaper. His spare dollars and hours are devoted to developing an amazing knowledge of the world, and physical skills like fencing, swimming and judo. Beneath the innocuous façade of a proof-reader he is really a highly trained athlete.

Hiram in 'The Adventure of the Misguided Missile'

In reality, Wally is an outdoorsman at heart. He swims a lot, walks a lot and spends as much time as he can in the open. Few things establish this trait like his love for motorcycles. His friends know him as a competent cyclist, one who can take his cycle cross country, after the roads leave off. "That's the Hiram Holliday in me," Wally laughs.

Cox was born Dec 6, 1924 in Detroit. Both his parents were writers and Wally explains, "we lived in the country until the money ran out, then moved back to the city to recoup. I like the country best."

The Return

Following his discharge from the Army, Wally returned to New York University where he had enrolled before World War II. Like other GIs, he wasn't sure what he wanted to do. Had he followed the findings of his aptitude tests, though, he might still be hand-fashioning jewellery for a livelihood. The tests said he should study arts and crafts and he did, giving them up when he found the field limited.

Wally's career took a turn when friends, after hearing his hilarious monologues at parties, urged him to try acting, "I did, "Wally recalls, "and promptly failed."

After a screening of the pilot for critics the reviews started to appear:

"It's almost impossible to predict the success or failure of a new TV series, but it looks as if NBC will have a winner this fall with *The Adventures of Hiram Holliday*.

I've seen the first of the half hour films and found it amusing and well done...

NBC and producer Phil Rapp have cast Wally Cox as the redoubtable Hiram, and I don't think they could have made a better choice. Certainly no one looks more like a Milquetoast than Cox. The contrast and paradox of his appearance played against his heroic exploits should give the new TV series an almost foolproof element of attraction for most viewers.

If all this sounds a little crazy and hokey, you're right. Of course it is played for comedy, and most of the time Cox is able to prevent things from flying completely out of bounds.

Gallico's original Hiram was a much more serious chap and in his fictional day he was busy thwarting Nazis and winning the war. Producer Rapp's plan to turn the series into a comedy is sound but he will have to restrain himself. Half the charm of watching Cox's Hiram is going to come from the viewers at least partially believing that Hiram just possibly might be able to do some of these things."[23]

"Wally Cox is a quick, taut, perfectly controlled comic, undersized and bespectacled, who showed brilliantly how the two sides of Hiram's character merge. Hiram's successes come when ordinary life takes the form for which his dream-hero self constantly prepares him and which he therefore does not find surprising. He can always deal with an alarming situation and can always explain it modestly and confidently."[24]

---

[23] Los Angeles Mirror-News, 30 August, 1956 by Hal Humphrey

[24] Birmingham Post, 3 August 1960

The show debuted on Wednesday 3 October, 1956 at 8pm replacing the Martha Roundtree current affairs show *Press Conference*. Production would run until January 1957. Bob Hull of the *Herald-Express*[25] paid the set a visit:

"Mr Peepers went off the air for a variety of reasons, including a lack of sponsor. Very serious you know." Wally told us the other day on the set "But my character seems to get a large spread in the Hiram Holliday thing. We do so many things in much more broad comedy."

To date Wally's show has become something the like the first season of the Phil Silvers shows—a program much discussed the day after its showing.

"I'm not worried about ratings," Wally pointed out to us "They're not too indicative. All I want to do is a show I will enjoy doing and people will enjoy seeing."

Wally did the Peepers show live in New York and the change to film for the Holliday adventures gladdens his heart. "So much more time to perfect things," he said. "Well cheerio! I've got to learn a Swiss yodelling call for this next scene."

But not everything was going according to plan. Before the show had debuted, Phil Rapp raised an issue with both the network and the sponsor. He didn't like the laugh track that NBC had insisted on dubbing on to the show. Young & Rubicam were, initially, very neutral on it and performed some further audience tests to see if there was any benefit with or without the laughter. They sent him a memo with the results in early September:

> Two Hiram Holliday pilot films were presented before the Y&R Audience Jury: one on 24 May 1956 with laugh track, the other on 6 September 1956 without laugh track. The May 24 jury received an overall enjoyment rating of 63 and the September 6 Jury received an overall enjoyment rating of 62. The overall enjoyment rating for all programs tested to date is 59 and the overall comedy average is 61. The difference of one point in overall enjoyment rating is not significant.
>
> The likes and dislikes concerning the show itself are about the same. 23% of the September Jury liked Wally Cox and 20% of the May Jury liked Cox. The May Jury had 3% of the Jurors (two Juror) who mentioned the disliking the canned laughter.

---

25 14 October 1956

According to these findings there was no really significant difference between the two versions of the program.

So in short, as the letter accompanying the memo said: "Because there is no significant evidence from this test to indicate that a non-laugh track version would be more successful, we feel at this time there should be no change from the policy of using a laugh track. It is our understanding that the laugh tracks for Hiram Holliday are made by recording actual audience reactions at a screening of each film. It is our belief that this is the closest way of achieving the feeling of the presences of a studio audience if the show cannot actually be filmed before an audience."

By the end of October, Rapp, having secured the backing of the star of the show went public with his battle and *Sponsor* magazine[26] noted that:

> Phil Rapp, producer-director of *The Adventures of Hiram Holliday*, wants the laugh tracks eliminated from the eight episodes of this series remaining in the can. Siding with him on this issue is the star of the program, Wally Cox. Their case: the show is basically satire, not farce comedy, and will gain a better reception if offered as such.
>
> Sponsor General Foods and agency Young & Rubicam apparently don't agree, want the laugh track left in.

Even *The Hollywood Reporter*, in their first review of the show, commented on the laugh track:

"We saw a preview of 'The Adventures of Hiram Holliday' with Wally Cox and predict a long healthy run. The laugh track is horrible and some of the pacing is frenetic but the Walter Mitty character who conquers the world is a wonderful symbol for frustrated viewers."[27]

But, sadly, there were signs that their prediction of a long and healthy run might not come true. By mid-October, with the show having been on air for just a couple of weeks, there was already a hint of trouble. General Foods had sponsored four half hour shows that season—*Zane Grey Theater*, *77th Bengal Lancers*, *West Point* and, of course,

---

26 27th October 1956
27 13 September 1956

Hiram Holliday—and it stretched their budget too far. They started looking for co-sponsors for any of those shows (but ultimately found none).

The favourable press kept on coming though: *Television Digest* named the show as one of the "ten best bets for TV hits" alongside the well-remembered *Playhouse 90* and the not-so-well-remembered *Washington Square*, *Air Power* and *Odyssey*. A couple of weeks later it refined its choices and noted that Hiram Holliday was getting critical acclaim alongside *Playhouse 90* and Walter Winchell.

However whilst favourable press is great, what really matters is the ratings and *The Adventures of Hiram Holliday* didn't stand a chance of finding an audience for it was up against two ratings juggernauts, *Disneyland* on ABC and *The Arthur Godfrey Show* on CBS (Arthur Godfrey was a very popular broadcaster and entertainer, Walt Disney, I guess you might have already heard of). Two weeks into its run and it was firmly lagging third in the ratings, with Disneyland getting ratings of 23.3, Arthur Godfrey getting 15 and Hiram getting just 7.3

The rumors started: Eric Stigler from Chicago ad agency MacFarland, Aveyard and Co. wrote to Eric Ebel, a vice-president at General Foods, in late October:

> Dear Mr Ebel:
>
> Like they say, "I'm not the 'Letter-to-the-Editor' type." In fact, the last time I wrote something like this was when they threatened to take "Mr Peepers" off the air, four or five years ago. Apparently a few score thousands of others agreed with me in their letters of protest… and "Mr Peepers" remained on TV (for, was it, 3 seasons?) to the delight of millions.
>
> Now I hear ugly, nasty, vicious rumors that "The Adventures of Hiram Holliday" is headed for oblivion. And this before barely the third program in the series had been telecast.
>
> To you, and to Mr Casey of your TV co-ordinating department, I say:
> <u>Gentlemen, if there is a particle of truth to this rumor…you have no idea of the mistake you're making!</u>

The Return

As a possessor of something of sixth sense of discrimination regarding comedy…based on years of experience in comedy, gag and special material writing…I immodestly admit to knowing the Good and the Bad in the preservation of humor in almost every form.

Now I say this: "The Adventures of Hiram Holliday" <u>given its chance</u> will prove to be one of the warmest, gayest, wittiest, most charming , <u>most popular</u> comedy hits of the season. And it will mean a rebirth of Wally Cox on television.

The premiere on which the series is based is one of undeniable power and charm. To take an unassuming, timid character-aspect and have it so disarmingly cloak a latent athletic prowess and predilection for deeds of derring-do—combining the most outstanding attributes of Superman, Steve Canyon and Douglas Fairbanks (Senior) – is to provide a theme idea that is nigh-perfect.

It is "The Secret life of Walter Mitty" developed and advanced a hundred fold. It combines the best elements of Robin Hood, The Mark of Zorro and The Lone Ranger, and invests them in a character who, in Wally Cox, appears at the outset closer to Mr Average than anyone on TV today. Then in reaches its point of crowning achievement in the superb writing and direction of Mr Phillip Rapp (incidentally, just for the record, I do not personally know either Mr Cox or Mr Rapp).

And if you want to get Freudian about it, this business of self-identification with the protagonist of a story is in itself enough to guarantee its success among the millions of potential male viewers from six to eighty-six. (I won't go into the combined mother/fair-maiden-in-distress attachment the gals of the nation will automatically have for Hiram—in this particular writing).

20 years ago I perceived the spark in his style that has made Phil Silvers the fair haired boy of comedy last and this season. I caught

George Gobel at Helsing's Vodvil Lounge here in Chicago shortly after World War II and pronounced him merely great. His five minute bit in the movie Tars and Spars twelve years ago told me Sid Caesar also possessed this multi-million-dollar comedy flair.

But this is no run down of my perceptive abilities. I merely state these facts to prove that I'm qualified to judge comedy and comedy-programs professionally…and I say "Hiram Holliday" is the Year's Greatest. Give it its head. It may not get precisely the same type of audience as "I love Lucy" and "Oh Susanna" but it will claim, I sincerely predict, a huge following of the type that knows, understands and enjoys good clean, warm, fanciful, entertaining comedy.

Watch and see."

Around the same time, Phil Rapp heard from the sponsor, who'd kept an eye on how the show was developing:

"Now that we have had time to see a number of Hiram Holliday's and read some more, and gather multiple opinions, including those of the bitterest newspaper critics, several positive suggestions have emerged. I hope that you will be able to make a journey to New York sometime soon so that we can discuss these at greater length. Meanwhile, I leave you with two suggestions –

1. Pace

The comment from the most vocal and discerning people which seems to hit home the most is the slowness of the first half of each of the scripts that has been presented on the air. It is their feeling that too much time is spent developing character and dwelling on minute reactions on the part of Wally. When the action finally takes place it is usually superb but so whirlwind the reviewer doesn't have much time to savour it. More time spent on action earlier in the script should pay dividends.

2. Wally Cox

I, in particular, have been concerned about the references in the paper to Wally Cox rather than HIRAM HOLLIDAY. You and I know that he is just an actor cast in a very important part but this impression is apparently not apparent to critics or viewers. If one were to cast this part ideally, it would probably be with someone who is physically more robust and possibly better looking. However, since we both agreed form the beginning that Wally Cox was excellent in the part and since we have made this decision, it is probably incumbent on us to make him more Hiram Holliday and less Wally Cox. Since his physical equipment is certainly adequate, you may want to show more scenes with Wally indicating his actual strength in order to further the believability of his exploits.

As you can see, I am frustrated by the limitation of the give and take for specific examples in this kind of discussion. I think perhaps the discussion of with-or-without laugh track could be handled with a fast pace affecting the philosophy of the entire series. Since it will be difficult for me to get to the Coast in the near future, I hope that you can arrange to come to New York and we can develop these points further."

Rod Erickson, a vice-president of Young & Rubicam wrote to Rapp on 19 December:

"Let us assume for the moment that professional people, intellectuals and industry leaders have enthusiastically accepted everything you are doing with 'Hiram Holliday.' Let us also assume that the basic premise of this series is potentially tops—the little man who, self-taught, can accomplish great physical and mental feats, should be the idol of everyone. We must, therefore, conclude that the show has been too good. The satire, the subtleties, the play on languages and names, will go down in the annals of telecasting as a superb bit of writing, but the show, as it stands now, will go down in the rating books as a commercial failure."

"…most of the scripts lack enough humorous physical action distributed throughout the body of the shows. Let's use the 'Swiss Titmouse' as an example…there is an overwhelming amount of repetition of pattern and plot from show to show."

He went on to highlight the contrived nature of plot structure, "...when the policemen suddenly appear from nowhere the audience doesn't see this as burlesquing the formula, but rather contributing to it." He went on to suggest that Rapp forsake the writing and directing and concentrate on being executive producer "in order to give you ample time to develop a new version of a great idea."

Sponsor magazine made the point that it wasn't just Hiram Holliday that was in trouble, sitcoms in general seemed out of favour:

"In the self-analysis the network TV fraternity is conducting on this year's programs, the new situations comedies definitely show up as a week spot. Not one has made any headway in the ratings.

Why? Situation comedy was one of radio's most durable and reliable props. Knowledgeable admen think they can spot this common current deficiency: The central characters in the TV comedies lack roots – ties to family, group or romance that make them emerge from the screen as real."

The magazine went on to name the main offenders as *Hey Jeanie*, *The Brothers*, *Oh, Susannah*, *Stanley* and of course, *The Adventures of Hiram Holliday* as the main offenders.

NBC were still supporting Messrs Rapp and Holliday. Phill Rapp met with NBC executive and former radio producer Thomas A. McAvity at the end of October:

> "I am glad we had the chance to meet last night and discuss the show in general and I want to reiterate what I said, which is that I think you're doing a great job and I have a genuine belief that the show will be a hit.
>
> With respect to the laugh track, I would only like to say again that I have never yet seen a comedy played successfully on television without laughter – whether it be live or film. I realise there is a great deal of criticism about laugh tracks in general, and I agree with most of it. I think the solution lies not in eliminating the laugh track, but rather in doing the track better – which you are doing. Laughter coming on top of lines without the accompanying projection by the actors seemingly topping the laughter always sounds phony. You and I know that this is a matter of direction. I do agree that on occasions where underscoring

is used, it is possible to do away with laughter, and I think the choice of where you have underscoring and where you have laughter will have to rest with you. I'm afraid I do not agree with Rod's observation that the laugh track tends to slow up the show; not do I agree that a laugh should only be used where there is a particularly funny situation or line. I think that many times a small laugh or chuckle is as important as a big laugh. It's a matter of punctuation and pace, and there is nothing more deadly, particularly to an actor like Wally Cox, than to be seemingly funny and have no laughter accompanying him. I will certainly trust your judgement on the use of laughter, provided we understand each other as I am sure we do."

They had, naturally, undertaken a large PR campaign to launch the show in October with adverts running in all the major newspapers in all the major markets and they followed it up with another ad campaign in those papers at the end of the month. Plus:

"For the October 3rd premiere and through the program of November 21, NBC has scheduled 96 announcements for Hiram Holliday. These promos on the full network gained an estimated 684,000,000 ARB viewer impressions and used network airtime worth $513,000 HIRAM HOLLIDAY will continue to receive strong network air support whenever possible.

A comprehensive kit of audience promotion materials was sent to all stations well in advance of the premiere date. These kits contain the items the stations they have told us they use most…items such as slides, ad mats, photographs, picture mats, air announcements, feature stories and program notes.

In addition to this pre-premiere mailing, special announcements for HIRAM HOLLIDAY are sent to stations each week via our Mail-O-Gram service. Also, film stations for trailers, and for the network, were made and distributed."[28]

The letters continued:

"Hurray for Hiram Holliday! This is the best comedy to appear on television since the Phil Silvers show. Wally Cox is the only actor capable of playing our hero, Hiram. My family hasn't laughed so much since Sgt. Bilko first appeared on TV."[29]

---

28 Letter to Rapp, 21 November 1956
29 Letter from Ray Cross, Buffalo, NY

As did the favourable coverage:

"In a town filled with actors whose egos run rampant across backgrounds of pure ham, Wally Cox is not only an anomaly but downright retiring.

Since coming to Hollywood six months ago to star in the new NBC TV series "Hiram Holliday" Wally hasn't been seen in a nightclub, at a movie premiere or even judging a beauty contest.

He takes his life in his hands every time he walks down the street because he can't see five feet ahead without his glasses. Wally leaves the spectacles in his pocket since he found out that most people fail to recognise his unbespectacled phiz.

This yen to steer clear of autograph hounds and other well-wishers does not stem from a dislike of his fellow man. Wally is simply embarrassed and uncomfortable by such adulation and never knows quite what to say.

I pointed out to him that such deportment is considered phony in Hollywood where many actors get sore lips from tooting their own horns.

"I know," says he, "but so far I've gotten by with it and haven't caused too much disturbance. I think the fact that I did "Peepers" on TV for three seasons has helped. People still look upon me as that shy little schoolteacher, so this seems to account for my actions."

Wally's reading is confined to National Geographic, Scientific American, American Natural History magazines and the Sunday news summary in the New York Times. He refuses to read the show business trade papers, which the average actor devours before he's had his orange juice.

"I don't want to get interested in the ratings and reviews of TV shows. It would only cause me to have emotional experiences which I can do without. After all, I'm just a visitor on this planet, and I want to enjoy it as much as I can," says the philosophical Wally.

If any of this makes Wally Cox sound like an oddball or spook, it may be because he is currently living in a town where sane attitudes are considered gauche and even slightly unhealthy.

When Wally leaves the studio where his Hiram Holliday series is filmed, he forgets show business and all that goes with it. He and his wife watch TV only occasionally. Wally has a theory that ultrasonic humming sounds from some of the circuits in a TV set have an irritating effect on the human nervous system.

Wally plans to quite the acting profession five years from now and become a playwright. He wants to move to the country, preferably in Connecticut "where the seasons are conventional and I can see some greenery – I like trees and streams."

It may be a while before Wally gets back to those trees and streams he's dreaming about. His Hiram Holliday series is beginning to catch on, despite the fact it bucks the formidable "Disneyland" in most key cities. The role of a milquetoast character who has the ingenuity of Superman and the courage of a bull is made to order for Wally.

Hiram Holliday also has the advantage of appealing to two types of audiences— those who take it literally and those who see the satire in most situations.

Of all the new comedy series which have bowed on TV this season "Holliday" is far the best of the lot.

Another good thing about it is that success couldn't happen to a nicer guy than Wally Cox."[30]

In December *Billboard* magazine decreed the show was the top-rated sitcom amongst men, beating out the likes of *Phil Silvers*, *I Love Lucy* and the *Life of Riley* amongst others. Women though, weren't so keen it seems, for it ranked no. 8, being beaten by shows such as *Burns & Allen* and *I Love Lucy*.

Hiram and his trusty weapon of choice

---

30 The Pittsburgh Press, 9 December 1956

A few weeks into its run it was clear that whilst everyone liked *The Adventures of Hiram Holliday* it couldn't find a big enough audience given the competition on the other two channels. In mid-November General Foods asked NBC if they could find another time slot for Hiram, saying they were convinced that Mondays at 8 to 8:30pm was too early because " too many youngsters in the East and Midwest are still in control of the sets at that early time". The problem, which was immediately obvious to most, was that if they shifted Hiram from competing against the ratings powerhouses on the other channels, another show would have to take its place and probably would do worse than Hiram.

By the end of the year it was public knowledge that NBC were looking for alternate sponsorship not just for Hiram, but for another eight shows; *Roy Rogers*, *Steve Allen*, *NBC News*, *77th Bengal Lancers*, *Meet the Press* and *Wells Fargo*.

It wasn't good news for Hiram at the start of 1957 either. General Foods announced at the end of January that they were pulling their sponsorship from the show in favour of becoming an alternating sponsor—alongside American Tobacco—of *Tales of Wells Fargo*, a new half hour show that would debut on NBC in March of that year. A couple of days later that bad news was compounded by the latest ratings which showed Hiram getting solidly beaten; *Disneyland* on ABC was getting a 28.0 rating, *The Arthur Godfrey Show* on CBS was getting 21.4 and Hiram was trailing a long way behind with a rating of just 10.4

No sponsor, last in the ratings, Hiram's future was bleak.

Word of Hiram's impending demise spread and NBC started receiving letters from viewers, lots of letters from viewers. This sample, from Phillip Nicholson of California:

"Dear Sirs,

I have heard, via *TV Guide*, that Hiram Holliday is going off the air. In my opinion it is one of the best shows on television. I suggest you move it to an earlier time slot and try again. I'm sure that the children would learn to love it as much as I do.

Please don't let it go off the air. I have watched every show and I think it is the best program on television. It is most unusual and humorous and Wally Cox is wonderful in the lead role."

Mrs. Stoner of Clinton, Tennessee, wrote, "It's hard to tell which one we enjoy most. Your TV program or your Instant Coffee. I'm not much of a TV fan, but I drop everything I'm doing, no matter what, to watch *Hiram* (we like Joel, too)—that Hiram, so sweet looking, that innocent stare, and he always wins out—no matter what he gets into—that look on his face is what gets me— where in this world did you find such a guy—he's perfect for that part."

California Productions also got a generous mailbag:

"To whom it may concern:

Hiram Holliday is the most delightfully satiric spoof on TV thus far. My husband and I watch it regularly and thoroughly enjoy it.

We hope that we may be able to continue to do so. We hope that it won't be taken off the air.

We have become great fans of Wally Cox and Ainslie Pryor and of course our admiration extends to Philip Rapp and Richard Powell.

(My husband particularly enjoys dining while watching this show because "Joel Smith" eats with such relish that it inspires his appetite.)"[31]

Many years before a letter-writing campaign saved *Star Trek* there was a co-ordinated effort to save Hiram. A form letter was circulated and fans inundated NBC with this:

"Dear Sir:

I have been to movies that have certainly raised the value of TV stock in my estimation; but now it is my pleasure to return to the movies after reading that certain, wholesome family programs are going to be taken off the air.

My family is very disturbed that Hiram Holliday is going to be replaced.

I sincerely hope that every effort is being made by those who care for wholesome entertainment to retain this program."

Hiram's guardian angel, Phil Rapp, responded to many of the letters:

"Dear Mrs Dibble,

I am deeply touched by your encouraging letter regarding Hiram Holliday. At this moment I'm doing everything in my power to find another sponsor and I have implicit faith that Hiram will come back and remain on the air for a long time.

---

31 Letter dated 27 February 1957 from Beatrice Williams of New York

Please do write again,
Sincerely
Philip Rapp"

So Mrs Dibble did...
"Dear Mr Rapp,

--and I thank you. In this jittery era when there is too little freedom from pressure...TV programs like Hiram Holliday, Noah's Ark, Bishop Sheen (and I am a protestant) are what the nations nerves need. It could be overdone, but give the public at least one daily program like yours or Noah's Ark and I'll betcha lots of folks could throw away their tranquilizer pills...to say nothing of the better attitude it might encourage in our young hoodlum element. There are too few opportunities in these days of high pressure for people of any age to get acquainted with the real fun there is in the soothing but interesting programs like yours. After all, who wants caviar and screwdrivers as a steady diet...which is the equivalent of our lives and recreation today! I don't mean that Hiram puts them to sleep...he just leaves them in a more peaceful and relaxed mood.""

Even the news in mid-January that "NBC-TV's Hiram Holliday has been named one of the two most unique new programs and one of the three best comedy film series of the season this week in the Eighth Annual Poll of television editors, critics and columnists conducted by *Television Today and Motion Picture Daily* for *Fame Magazine*,"[32] couldn't stop the end of Hiram Holliday.

The official letter of cancellation came on 31 January 1957. The last network broadcast aired 27 February 1957 and was the twenty-second episode, entitled 'The Adventure of the Misguided Missile'. It was replaced in the schedule by *Masquerade Party*, a long running game show where a panel of celebrities would have to guess the identity of another celebrity who was heavily made up or in costume.

On hearing news that the show had been cancelled Donald Freeman of the *San Diego Union* ran a tribute to the hard luck of the show. Quoting Phil Rapp, it stated that the show didn't have a chance due to its placement up against rival networks' *Disneyland* on ABC and Arthur Godfrey on CBS. "In any other time spot," said Rapp, "I'm convinced *Hiram Holliday* would have doubled its rating." *Mr. Peepers* had

---
32 NBC Press Release, 17 January 1957

followed the same curse, being up against Jack Benny and *What's My Line?* at various times. Still, both series kept a resolute, dedicated following. "Actually," wrote Dave Freeman, "when such shows are choked off, it is television itself which suffers the most grievous loss because its scope, which could be so vast, becomes that much narrower, its potential that much less fulfilled."[19]

Twenty-six episodes had in fact been completed and the cost of stopping production, excluding financial commitments to Rapp, was estimated at $54,000, of which $32,000 was for studio time which had already been booked and contracted. Rapp initially intended to complete the first run of thirty-nine episodes, which would make the show more appealing in syndication, but NBC would not sanction any further production.

Chapter Four: The Episodic Adventures of Hiram Holliday

The synopses detailed below are those issued by NBC in order to promote the show both at home and abroad. The BBC synopsis is that issued by the BBC and published in their TV guide, the *Radio Times*. The story is a more detailed breakdown of what happens in the episode.

1. **The Adventure of the Attaché Case**
Script No. 101
Production No. 2601
Sponsored by Sanka
Release date: 3rd October 1956
BBC first run: 2nd August 1960 at 18:50, repeated 22nd January 1961

Written, produced and directed by Philip Rapp
Cinematography by Lester Shorr
Cast: Wally Cox (Hiram Holliday), Ainslie Pryor (Joel Smith), Thurston Hall (Harrison Prentice), Joanna Mariani (Gaby), Maurice Marsac (Fencing Instructor), Lita Milan (Marlene), Raymond Bailey (Sharpe), Robert Boon (Steward), Noel Drayton (Major), Wilton Graff (Captain)

Synopsis:
Wally Cox, armed with bumbershoot and a bland contempt for danger, grapples with some sinister forces on shipboard.

Hiram (Cox), a mild-mannered newspaper proof-reader, possessed of a great physical prowess and an encyclopaedic mind, sets out on a round-the-world tour, his reward from his publisher for sparing the newspapers a libel suit in discovering a misplaced comma. Accompanying him, to chronicle his adventures, is reporter Joel Smith (Ainslie Pryor).

Before the liner is well out to sea, Hiram is involved in a spy ploy to steal dispatches from a US emissary. The spies are a sultry female and the ship's fencing instructor who select Hiram as a dupe. They arrange for a ferocious lion to escape in order to divert the passengers while they carry out their plot. But they have underestimated Hiram—wizard fencer, sultry female, ferocious lion and all!

Thurston Hall as the publisher, and Lita Milan and Maurice Marsac as the spies will appear in various roles throughout the filmed series. Other featured players are Wilton Graff and Philip Tonge.

Phil Rapp is writer, producer and director. The teleplays are based on the Paul Gallico stories that appeared in Cosmopolitan Magazine.

BBC Synopsis:
The invincible Hiram foils the plot of an international gang to seize some important documents on board ship and proves that an umbrella can be very useful in a tight corner.

Story:
Steven Sharpe, top trouble shooter in the US Foreign Affairs Department, is sailing across the Atlantic on the liner Brittannique. He is enjoying a cup of tea when he hears shooting; a steward advises him it's the finals of the passenger pistol competition. Sharpe, we discover, has a small leather dispatch case attached to his wrist and is being guarded by a secret service agent.

At the shooting gallery on the promenade deck Major Spitalfield-Neves, famous adventurer-explorer-soldier-of-fortune-big-game-hunter, over six feet tall with dashing, piercing eyes, shows off his skill to an appreciative audience of (mainly) young ladies. He is a very good shot however his ego takes a bashing when the steward points out he is almost as good as Mr Holliday, who shot ten bullets through just the one hole.

In the ships hospital a surgeon had just finished operating. The Major dashes in to offer his blood but it's not needed for what was a very tricky operation has just finished. The Major congratulates the surgeon but discovers that the doctor didn't perform the surgery, Hiram Holliday did.

Below decks, where the livestock are normally kept, are a group of lions and tigers. The Major is holding forth to a group of people telling the story of how he managed to capture one of the lions alive. The captain and a couple of crewmen interrupt the Major's tale as they dump a mechanical device overboard…it was a bomb, designed to eliminate Steven Sharpe, and it was disarmed with a shoe-horn and a sail-maker's needle by Hiram Holliday. The Major is exasperated wondering just who on earth is Hiram Holliday!

Joel Smith, also on the boat, tells us that five days ago Hiram Holliday was an obscure proof-reader for the *New York Sentinel*. "For fifteen years he hoarded his salary and went to fencing sale and shooting school, took lessons in foil, epee, saber, pistol and rifle. He learned to ride, swim, box, ski and fly a plane…and when he couldn't afford instruction he resorted to books, developing an encyclopaedic knowledge embracing every art and skill from surgery to savate…He might have remained a proof-reader the rest of his life, except that last week, just by transposing a misplaced comma, he saved the paper from a million dollar libel suit." That earned him a five thousand dollar bonus, a promotion to special reporter, and a one year around the world expenses paid trip. Prentice sent Smith along with him, to write a series of stories about Hiram Holliday.

Hiram heads to the ship's gym where he meets the gym instructor, Franz Dupree. Hiram is looking for someone to fence with and Dupree offers his services. After an exciting sword fight Hiram manages to draw blood on Dupree's shirt. Hiram is apologetic, but Dupree dismisses it as Hiram leaves.

The steward catches up with Dupree and it becomes clear that they, along with a lady called Marlene, have a plan to relieve Steve Sharpe of his dispatch case. There is a masquerade ball tonight and they'll create a diversion to get all the passengers back to their quarters.

Hiram is getting ready for the ball as Joel, dressed as a swami and wearing a jewelled turban, goes to call for him.

The ballroom is heaving, full of masked people. The Major is dressed as a cavalier, the ship's doctor wearing a convict suit and the envoy—dispatch case still attached—in tails. Dupree and Marlene, dressed as a cat, are also in attendance though Sharpe's bodyguard is not, for he has been dumped over the side of the boat a hundred miles back and replaced by one of their men. They are looking for a dupe as part of their scheme and Marlene favors Hiram, who arrives at the ball dressed as Mickey Mouse.

Marlene asks Hiram to dance the tango and although Hiram says he's only read about it, never practiced it, we discover just how good his reading has been. He is soon a master of the dance floor.

Sharpe retires to his room and hands the case over to his bodyguard. The goon, by way of thanks, knocks him unconscious with the butt of his gun. The steward, meanwhile, creeps down to the animal cages and lets one of the lions loose.

With a lion on the loose the ballroom is quickly evacuated, and everyone told to return to their quarters however in the melee Hiram's glasses are knocked off and by the time he finds them he is the only one left.

He makes his way back to his room and soon there's a loud rapping on his door. It's Marlene who makes out she has lost her way and is terrified. Hiram offers to help her find her room but Marlene wants to stay in his…and she needs a drink. Whilst

Hiram is on the phone ordering drinks Marlene sneaks into his bedroom and hides the dispatch case in his luggage.

The lion sneaks into Hiram's room whilst Hiram is on the phone and has his back turned. As the lion approaches him he slowly hangs up the phone. Marlene appears from the bathroom, terrified. Hiram stares the lion down.

Major Spitalfield-Neves accompanied by a few men and, with whip drawn and gun in hand, makes his way downs the corridor outside of Hiram's room when he hears a roar. He throws open the door of Hiram's cabin ready to shoot…only to discover a content lion with its head in Hiram's lap. Whilst the Major encourages the lion back to his cage the Captain congratulates Hiram on his bravery and departs, leaving Hiram and Marlene in the room. The drinks arrive and with Marlene's encouragement Hiram discovers a liking for champagne.

The morning after Hiram wakes to find Marlene in bed with him. She tells him that after they'd drunk the champagne the Captain married them. Hiram sniffs at the champagne glass from last night and concludes he was drugged, which Marlene admits. She also confesses her involvement with the plot to get the dispatch case as Dupree arrives with a rapier; their plane has arrived and they are due to make their escape.

Hiram grabs his umbrella and a fight ensues, umbrella versus sword. The fight moves onto the deck and a smart move by Hiram ensures that Dupree goes sailing over the rail and into the water.

The captain rushes up to thank Hiram, followed by sailors who have a firm grip on the crooked steward and Marlene. As he gushes his thanks the Major also arrives to finally meet the man who beat him on the shooting range, who performed the operation, dismantled the bomb, and subdued the lion…

Notes:

Pilots can be notoriously last minute things with producers and other creative staff focused on trying to make a sellable product. The final version of the revised shooting script was dated 17th March 1956. Production started ten days later on stage 4 at California Studios. They rehearsed all day March 26th and from the 27th through to the 30th shot roughly a quarter of the seventy-nine scenes each day. Most days started at 8.45am and ran until 6.55pm with an hour for lunch. The two main stars—Cox and Pryor—were in make-up at 7.45am and on set just half an hour later. The two lion trainers cost $35 each along with 1.5 hours overtime. The budget for this pilot was $45,725 though they ended up going over budget and bringing it in for a little over $50,000.

John Bushnell, assistant manager of the NBC continuity acceptance department, wrote to Phil Rapp on 19 March 1956 having read the pilot script:

"Regarding this script, please consider the following:

Be sure that Sharpe, the envoy, does not closely resemble any high-level official in government or close confidant of the President, such as Bernard Baruch or John Foster Dulles. Such a "take-off" would be in extremely dubious taste with regard to foreign relations and public relations.

On page 12, suggest deletion of comment regarding sex life of the tulip. Although somewhat mild, it will be considered a sex joke by a percentage of viewers and can easily be changed.

On page 17 please delete "bandaids". We have been requested to avoid generic use of this trade name as sufficient generic usage will cause loss of the exclusive trademark.

Page 20, be sure cat costume on Marlene is in good taste and not too form-revealing. In scene beginning on page 39, please do not show Marlene in bed and lose inference that she spent all night with Hiram. This includes opening shot and subsequent remarks such as languorous "good morning, darling", references to what he has "missed". Deletion of bed business will take care of his dismay at her getting up presumably without clothes on."

Joanna Mariani who plays Gaby in this episode was, for a short while, engaged to Wally Cox's good friend Marlon Brando. Also known as Josanne Mariani she was the daughter of a fisherman and a former model who'd met Brando in a New York nightclub at the age of 17. In late 1954—the year he won an Oscar for his role in *On the Waterfront*—he announced they were to be married however shortly after her appearance in this show they split. She later married a lawyer and moved back to Paris.

French actor Maurice Marsac, who played Dupree, was born in France in March, 1915. In the 1930s he worked in the French Embassy in London and served as a Captain in the French Army Reserves. During the War he served in the French Resistance before moving to the USA and starting work as an actor. His first role was as an uncredited French soldier in the 1943 film *Paris After Dark*. Often cast as a snooty continental he had a long career in film and television and went on to appear in shows such as *The New Avengers*, *The A Team* and *The Fall Guy*. He was also a nationally ranked croquet player. He died in May 2007 in California, less than three weeks after his wife of 55 years.

Lita Milan walked away from her acting career just a few years after her recurring role on this show. She was born Iris Maria Lia Menshall in Brooklyn, New York in 1933, to Polish-Hungarian parents. Her father, Albert Menschell, was a furrier who used to do bit parts in Hollywood pictures. She studied dance in her early years and after graduating from high school changed her name to Lita Milan, moved to Las Vegas and found work as a chorus girl. She also worked as a model and appeared in several magazines including *Night & Day* and *Photo*.

What she really aspired to was Hollywood and she got her break in 1954 when she won a role in the Louis Hayward TV series *The Lone Wolf*. Over the next few years she made a number of guest appearances in shows such as *Passport to Danger* and *Studio 57*. She combined these appearances with a number of film roles with her career perhaps reaching its peak in 1957 when she was cast as Paul Newman's leading lady in *The Left Handed Gun*.

But she gave it all up for love.

She fell for Ramfis Trujillo, the eldest playboy son and heir of Rafael Trujillo then dictator of the Dominican Republic. They married and moved to the Dominican Republic to be closer to his family. But Trujillo senior was assassinated in 1961 and the couple fled to Madrid, Spain, where they lived under the shelter of the dictator General Francisco Franco. Ramfis had inherited his father's ill-gotten gains and they lived a good life until eight years later when Ramfis died in a car crash. She then, to quote a number of newspapers, became "Spain's merry widow" and enjoyed a party lifestyle. However, she was living beyond her means and was last heard of living in a tiny apartment in Leganes, a small, ugly industrial town near Madrid. In recent years she gave an interview in which she said that marrying Ramfis and sacrificing her career had been a mistake for she thought she could have gone much further as an actress.

Trade paper *Variety* offered favourable comments on this first episode but also hit the nail on the head with regard to the problems the cast and crew might encounter:

"Wally Cox, Phil Rapp, NBC-TV and General Foods have come up with the first click of the new season, a raffish and outlandish comedy based on the Paul Gallico Cosmopolitan short story series. It's a case of perfect casting for Cox, who has been floundering for the right vehicle since the demise of "Mr Peepers", and as triplethreated by Phil Rapp as producer-director-writer, emerges as solid farce, probably the hardest type of comedy to get across the home screens.

If there are any kinks in Holliday's armour, they are the fact that it's placed at a competitive disadvantage – opposite "Disneyland" and the moot question of "how long can they keep it up?" The latter point refers to the fact that the opening episode was a fast-paced gambit that had more than its quota of situations and laughs. If Rapp and whomever he leans on for support can maintain the pace, he's a winner. There's still that "Disneyland" factor, of course, but from the looks of the new schedule there will be plenty of other time slots opening come January and NBC-TV can pick and choose if it decides to call Wednesday at 8 a total loss in the face of "Disneyland's" formidability.

The Gallico yarns are concerned with a Milquetoast proof-reader who has secretly perfected himself in all of the physical arts and who's sent on a year's round-the-world tour by the publisher as a reward for averting a libel suit by his corrections. First shipboard episode has Cox taming a lion, seeing through a romantic lure, winning a pistol match, defusing a time bomb and outwitting a spy ring and saving secret state papers for a Presidential envoy. He even parries the sword of a master fencer with his umbrella.

On the face of it, it's so much nonsense, but with the ludicrous figure and characterisation set by Cox it becomes hilarious nonsense. Supporting cast is fine, with Lita Milan representing the romantic interest with good comedy flair. Ainslie Prior a fine foil as the reporter sent along with Cox and Maurice Marsac exhibiting a good broad approach as the head spy.

Rapp, who apart from his triple-threating, also created the package does a topflight job in all three capacities and if he can keep it up he's an NBC hero. Series is being filmed by California National Productions, the recently expanded NBC subsidiary, and the quality is good, bespeaking a happy omen for the subsid."[33]

2. **The Adventure of the Lapidary Wheel**
Script No. 102
Production No. 2602
Sponsored by Jello

---

[33] Variety, 10 October 1956

Release date: 10th October 1956
BBC first run 3rd August 1960 at 18:50, repeated 29th January 1961
Written, produced and directed by Philip Rapp

The lovely Lita Milan playing the not always lovely Marlene

Cast: Wally Cox (Hiram Holliday), Ainslie Pryor (Joel Smith), John Abbott (Headmaster), John Alderson (Policeman), John Colicos (Thief), Pamela Light (Ada), Wilton Graff (Ship's Captain), Ben Wright (Museum Receptionist), Jared Brown

Synopsis:
A beautiful young temptress, a huge diamond and a king cobra all figure in this adventure. Hiram (Cox) is on the overnight train from London to Scotland and has a close brush with death when thieves, after the diamond, battle with him atop the moving train.

Pamela Light, Australian actress, appears as the temptress.

The cobra used in the story escaped during the filming and frightened many members of the cast. But not the intrepid Hiram. Cox wandered round the studio lot until the reptile was caught, then later agreed to do the snake-charming scene in the episode without the plate glass usually kept between actor and cobra.

BBC Synopsis:
Hiram arrives in Britain for the beginning of his trip around the world. On a train journey to Scotland he finds some travelling companions who become as interested in him as they are in a famous diamond.

Story:
An ocean liner crossing the north Atlantic has a problem which someone had to fix. The man in question has been overboard and under water for fourteen minutes, much to the amazement of everybody watching. Suddenly Hiram climbs aboard, he is the man in question and he's fixed the rudder. As Hiram goes to get out of his wet suit a lady asks the Captain who he was. The Captain tells her that was Hiram Holliday, the last of the romantic heroes...

In London Hiram visits a jewel merchants in search of a lapidary wheel. As Hiram waits for the shop assistant to return he gets talking to another customer, a headmaster, and Hiram explains that he wants to make a chess board with stones using the wheel. The headmaster has been admiring The Sorrow of Shahbandar, a 252-carat gemstone that is going back to India tomorrow.

Joel returns to their hotel room to discover Hiram hard at work using the lapidary wheel. When Joel queries that Hiram hasn't unpacked yet Hiram explains that he's going up to Scotland tonight to look at some rocks for his chessboard.

Later on the train up, Joel heads to the diner whilst Hiram tries to find an empty compartment. He finds one with just a Hindu gentleman in and leaves his luggage, going off to get Joel's case for him. As Hiram picks up Joel's case he bumps into a policeman and the case opens, revealing a bottle of whiskey.

Hiram settles into the compartment to wait for Joel and tries to make conversation with his fellow passenger, but the Hindu lurches forward, dead, revealing a knife in his back. Hiram calmly leaves his compartment, closes the door and goes in search of the policeman. Hiram explains everything to him but when they go back to Hiram's compartment the body has disappeared.

The policeman dismisses Hiram as a crank and goes back to his compartment. Hiram decides to investigate the apparently murdered man's luggage and opens a small basket, only to discover a cobra in it.

Hiram goes back to see the policeman but the policeman still thinks Hiram's a crank however he does go back to see the cobra. Hiram carefully pries the lid off the basket only to discover that cobra too has disappeared. The policeman returns to his seat in frustration.

The headmaster and two companions, Ernie and Ada, are in a nearby compartment watching the policeman return. As they talk it's clear they killed the Hindu whilst looking for the Shahbandar and threw his body off the train. The headmaster concludes Hiram must have the gem.

Whilst Ernie searches Hiram's compartment Ada keeps him distracted in the corridor. The dastardly duo walk away whilst Hiram discovers his compartment has been tossed. The headmaster visits Hiram who is still picking over the state of his compartment and introduces Ada and Ernie as his secretary and his Greek instructor.

As the headmaster gets to the point Ernie reveals he threw the Hindu off the train and draws his knife on Hiram. Ada spies the basket in the corner. The lid has been left off it and the cobra decides to explore its surroundings…

To calm it down Hiram improvises some music using his comb and a piece of paper but the cobra comes higher out of the basket and looks ready to strike. The headmaster starts to panic…but as Hiram plays a tune with his comb the cobra retreats into his basket and Hiram quickly replaces the lid.

Hiram picks up the snake in the basket and leaves the compartment, threatening the trio as he exits. He makes his way to see the policeman again but the policeman is resolutely cynical. Hiram tells him everything, including who murdered the Hindu. The bobby escorts Hiram back to his own compartment and tells him to stay put and not disturb him again.

A minute after the policeman leaves Ada visits Hiram and tells him she has the diamond and has double-crossed the headmaster. The headmaster appears holding a gun on Hiram and Ada. He demands the diamond but instead Hiram reaches for his umbrella and plugs the gun as it misfires. Hiram runs, closely followed by the headmaster. Ernie soon joins the chase and Hiram climbs outside the train carriage, running along the top of the train. Soon a fight ensues but Hiram and his umbrella manage to defeat the duo.

Notes:
The final revisions to the shooting script for this episode were done on the 16th July 1956. Total cost of this episode was \$42,575 of which \$7,985 was for the cast, \$3,580

was for the story, $1,325 for 'supervision' (presumably production management) and just $750 for the directing.

John Abbott, who plays the headmaster, was a fascinating man. Born in Stepney, London in June 1905 he made his stage debut in *Aurengzebe* in London at the age of 29 and quickly joined the Old Vic Company. Amongst numerous Shakespearean roles he played Claudius in *Hamlet* with Sir Laurence Olivier, Vivien Leigh and Alec Guinness at Denmark's Elsinore Castle. He made his film debut in 1937 and his Broadway debut in 1946. In the early days of the Second World War he worked at the British Embassy in Moscow. When it came time to leave, in 1941, he had to go via the United States where he was offered a part in Hollywood. He stayed there for the rest of his life.

Abbott was blacklisted during the communist scare of the early 1950s and for decades had no idea why. It turns out that Dalton Trumbo, one of the Hollywood Ten who was blacklisted, had written a 1935 novel about a character called John Abbott. When he'd been blacklisted he carried on writing pseudonymously using the names of characters from his stories. The real John Abbott—the actor—was removed from the blacklist when a producer who wanted to hire him fought his case.

Abbott went on to play roles in numerous TV shows from the 1950s through to the 1980s including *Star Trek*, *The Man From UNCLE*, *Perry Mason* and *Peter Gunn*. He died on 24 May 1996.

John Colicos, who played the other thief, was a Canadian actor born in December 1928. He began his acting career in 1946 on stage in Canada and built up substantial international stage experience before moving into films and television. He's probably best remembered now for his stint as Kor in the original *Star Trek* as well as *Star Trek: Deep Space Nine* but he also played Count Baltar in *Battlestar Galactica* as well as roles in shows such as *Mission: Impossible*, *Petrocelli* and *Wonder Woman*. He died in March, 2000 having returned to Toronto, Canada.

Twenty-six-year-old Pamela Light was a former model from Melbourne, Australia who gave up her modelling career to travel to America with her husband Jerry. This was her TV debut and she went on to have a number of small roles in shows such as *Alfred Hitchcock Presents*, *Studio 57* and *The George Burns and Gracie Allen Show* but by the mid-1960s the roles had stopped coming and she left the industry.

3. **The Adventure of the False Monarch**
Script No. 103
Production No. 2604
Sponsored by Sanka
Release date: 17th October 1956
BBC first run 4th August 1960 at 18:50, repeated 5th February 1961
Written, produced and directed by Philip Rapp

Cast: Wally Cox (Hiram Holliday), Ainslie Pryor (Joel Smith), Richard Aherne (Earl), Angela Greene (Queen of Rovakia), Thurston Hall (Harrison Prentice), John Wengraf (King's Aide)

Synopsis:
Wally Cox risks his life to save a kingdom by posing as the lookalike monarch who is an assassin's target.

Hiram is puttering about Scotland in search of lichens when an emissary of the visiting king of Rovakia enlist him as the monarch's double, neglecting to advise him of the danger. In his guise as the king, Hiram is invited to the gloomy castle of a bogus Scottish Earl who is actually the man assigned to slay the king. After several close calls Hiram reluctantly comes to the conclusion that the king—ipso facto Hiram—is a marked man.

A rousing Highland knife-dance, a dungeon torture chamber and a claymore-mace duel light up the gloomy castle.

BBC Synopsis:
Hiram interrupts the search for a rare lichen in Scotland in order to save the life of the King of Rovakia.

Story:
Hiram and Joel are in Scotland, staying at the Loch Dunoon Inn. Prentice discovers Joel eating dinner in the dining room, whilst Hiram is out—busy searching for lichens.

Making his way back into the inn Hiram bumps into Ulrich, a minister from a small middle-European country, who calls him 'your majesty' and seems confused. He gets Hiram to stay where he is and goes off to a room to see King Siegfried the

First, the Oxford educated King of Rovakia. Ulrich explains that he has the answer to their problem; they believe an attempt will be made on his life this weekend at Castle McConkie – they should send a double, Hiram, instead. They would keep this just between themselves and not tell the Queen.

Ulrich brings Hiram in and aside from a monocle and a royal crest on his robe, the resemblance is remarkable. He then goes on to persuade Hiram to take the king's place but, unsurprisingly, neglects to mention any possible attempt on the king's life. All Hiram wants by way of payment – to get to some of the lichens on the north wall of the castle, which the guards are currently preventing access to.

Hiram, dressed in a cutaway and with a row of ribbons, leads a procession through the dining room—passing by an astonished Joel and Mr Prentice. They are even more astonished when one of the waiters refers to him as "His majesty".

Hiram makes his way to McConkie Castle and meets the Earl of McConkie. But whilst Hiram is admiring one of the paintings an arrow narrowly misses him and hits the painting instead.

A banquet is given in the King's honour that evening; the entertainment includes a Scottish lass doing a sword dance and two kilted jugglers tossing knives up in the air. The Sword of McConkie hangs above Hiram's head; "tradition say that the sword shall only fall if the chair below is taken by a false monarch." Hiram moves quickly to avoid the sword as it falls but finds himself in the middle of the knife jugglers with knives being thrown all around him. He manages to catch them all and earns an enthusiastic round of applause.

As Hiram gets ready for bed he is joined by the Queen who, of course, is unaware of Hiram's resemblance to her husband. Meanwhile Joel and Prentice sneak along the castle wall trying to find out what Hiram is up to.

Hiram's conversation with the Queen is interrupted as Joel and Prentice are dragged into the hallway by a guard who is about to throw them in the dungeon.

Once they are locked up Hiram borrows a pin from the Queen, goes down to see them and picks the lock to set them free. They sneak into the torture chamber to hide from the guards but the door locks behind them and Hiram has lost his pin.

Then an open book and a candle suddenly float through the air towards them. Hiram believes they are suspended on wires but when he waves his hand around them, he finds no support whatsoever. The book is an account of the 13th McConkie beheaded in 1402, whose ghost now wanders around the castle...

A figure in chain mail and breastplate appears, carrying mace and walking towards them. The ghost takes a swipe at Hiram, who grabs a claymore to defend himself. In defeat the man in the chain mail reveals himself to be the Earl of McConkie who was being paid by the King's enemies. Ulrich and the police burst in and arrest the Earl.

Notes:
Total cost of this episode was $39,027.

Richard Aherne was an Irish actor born in March, 1911 in Dublin. He appeared in many films including the 1943 film *Sahara* with Humphrey Bogart and the 1956 classic *Around the World in Eighty Days*. He was sometimes credited as Richard Nugent to avoid confusion with the actor Brian Aherne. He died in 2002 in his home in Hollywood but was interred in his native Ireland.

Angela Greene was also born in Dublin, but ten years after her co-star. At the age of six she was adopted by her uncle and moved to Flushing, New York, where she grew up. She became a model for the Powers Agency and moved into acting with a number of uncredited roles in the mid-1940s. She played Tess Trueheart in the 1950 TV series of *Dick Tracy* as well as appearing in *Topper* and the Bernard Schubert produced *The Adventures of the Falcon* before meeting Hiram. She continued with the guest roles—a lot of guest roles—in many series until the mid-1970s. She died of a stroke in 1978, two weeks before what would have been her 57th birthday.

4.   **THE ADVENTURE OF THE HOLLOW UMBRELLA**
Script No. 104
Production No. 2603
Sponsored by Jello
Release date: 24th October 1956
BBC first run 8th August 1960 at 18:50, repeated 12th February 1961
Written, produced and directed by Philip Rapp
Directed by William H. Hole Jr.

Cast: Wally Cox (Hiram Holliday), Ainslie Pryor (Joel Smith), Stanley Adams (Garreaux), Eric Feldary (Wolfgang), Lita Milan (Marlene)

Synopsis:
Fleeing the police and dangerous villains, Wally Cox is forced to go into action as a nightclub apache dancer and a circus trapeze artist as he attempts to outwit a spy ring.

Wally, as the intrepid Hiram, travelling through Paris, picks up an umbrella believing it to be his. Inside the umbrella's hollow handle he finds a cryptic message which he has translated at a language school. The operators call police, because the message introduces the bearer as a foreign agent.

When the actual spy Garreaux (Stanley Adams) realizes that Hiram has the message, he enlists the help of Marlene (Lita Milan) and Wolfgang, a circus aerialist (Eric Feldary) in regaining the piece of paper.

As Hiram outwits police and spies, his reporter pal Joel (Ainslie Pryor) as usual, is oblivious to the excitement.

BBC Synopsis:
An innocent in Paris finds himself part of a high wire act.

Story:
Prentice becomes frustrated with Smith's failure to report on many of Holliday's adventures, caused by Smith being away at key opportunities coupled with Holliday's modesty in describing his encounters. He is sent with Holliday to Paris, where he yet again misses out on Holliday saving the French minister from a malfunctioning elevator. Holliday reveals he is in Paris on a truffle-hunting expedition. At a café, Holliday accidentally bumps into a bearded fellow and they accidentally switch umbrellas. The bearded man, Garreaux, meets with trapeze artist Wolfgang and Marlene, freed from prison after her earlier encounter with Holliday. They are working as spies delivering a secret message of great import hidden in the hollow handle of Garreaux's umbrella. However, they soon discover that they have Holliday's umbrella by mistake, and they vow to hunt down Holliday to retrieve the message.

Holliday discovers the hollow compartment inside the umbrella and the note within. It is written in the long-dead Etruscan language, which Holliday cannot translate. Smith believes this occurrence is of no importance and leaves on his own affairs, but Holliday is curious and takes the message to a language institute to be translated. The language professor, upon reading the message, is horrified by its contents and rushes to call the gendarmes to arrest Holliday, believing he is at the root of some dark conspiracy. Holliday, confused by this turn of events, returns to his apartment to find Garreaux and Marlene waiting for him. Garreaux asks that they return each other's umbrellas, but becomes angry when he finds the message is gone and holds Holliday at gunpoint to retrieve it. Holliday uses a trick to evade the gunfire and then knock Garreaux unconscious. Marlene claims that Garreaux's men will be after him and asks that he stay with her for the time being.

Hiram notices an autographed picture of Wolfgang on her mantle, recognising him from a poster he saw earlier. Marlene works as an exotic dancer in a café, and disguises Holliday so as to elude the gendarmes, although Hiram would rather turn himself in and explain everything. She has him act as her dance partner and attempts to covertly murder him with a knife, but Holliday thwarts her attempt, somewhat by accident."

She has Holliday act as his dance partner and attempts to covertly murder him with a knife, but Holliday thwarts her attempt, somewhat by accident. When the gendarmes enter, she takes him to the circus and makes him wear a rubber pig nose. Holliday is accidentally hoisted up to the trapeze with Wolfgang, and introduced as part of the act. Smith is in the audience and watches with terror as Holliday swings back and forth across the trapeze without a net to catch him. Wolfgang tries to kill Holliday by allowing him to fall, but he catches onto Wolfgang with the hook of his umbrella handle and evades falling to his death. Wolfgang then fences Holliday on a tightrope and knocks him off, but Holliday saves himself with a trampoline and manages to get away and set everything right. Smith interviews him later about the story and is dismayed to learn that Holliday ate the secret message to prevent it from being intercepted.

Notes:
Total cost of this episode was $46,403.

5.   **The Adventure of the Sea Cucumber**
Script No. 105
Production No. 2606
Sponsored by Sanka
Release date: 31st October 1956
BBC first run 9th August 1960 at 18:50, repeated 19th February 1961
Produced and directed by Phil Rapp
Written by Phillip Rapp, John Kohn and Bernard Drew

Cast:
Wally Cox (Hiram Holliday), Ainslie Pryor (Joel Smith), Sebastian Cabot (Gemmel), Murvyn Vye (Ship's Captain), Maria de Rosa (Natasha), Mark Dana (Nordstrom), Fred Cavens (Wang), Wim Sonneveld (Airport Desk Receptionist), Thurston Hall (Harrison Prentice)

Synopsis:
Wally Cox turns undersea frogman to foil foreign agents in "The Sea Cucumber".

The globe-trotting Hiram reaches Hong Kong and is mistaken by the agents for a spy hunter arrived to thwart an illegal arms shipment. The master spy (Sebastian Cabot) and his cohorts (Maria De Rosa and Fred Cavens) try to immobilize Hiram and attempt to seize the explosives sent to destroy the gun-runner ship.

They succeed instead in capturing the true counterspy (Mark Dana) who has secretly switched luggage with Hiram to keep the explosives from falling into wrong hands. Hiram dons the frogman's gear to reach the gun-loaded ship. Before he takes it off again he has accomplished several heroic missions.

Story:
Hiram and Joel are in Kuala-Lumpur and about to catch flight 32 to Hong Kong. Joel is worried about missing another story whilst Hiram is hopeful that his long search for a rare form of sea cucumber may come to an end whilst they're there. As they go to board they're followed by another occidental, a Mr Nordstrom who's also taking the flight. Once they've gone the attendant mysteriously phones a Hong Kong number to report there are only three occidentals on your flight so "you should encounter no difficulty in picking out your man."

In the Café of the Seven Lotus Blossoms in Hong Kong Gemmel hands over an envelope full of cash to a ship's captain. The Captain will be shipping arms for Gemmel, however someone has discovered his nefarious deed so Gemmel has arrange for the Captain to take a passenger, a passenger who arrives this afternoon on flight 32 but will not survive the whole of the boat journey. Gemmel tells Natasha and Wang that they will escort the man from flight 32 and make sure he gets on the boat.

Hiram and Nordstrom go through customs at the same time, their bags are remarkably alike. Gemmel points out Nordstrom to Natasha but she misunderstands and thinks he means Hiram. After that is made clear Wang and Natasha take Nordstrom away at gunpoint. In a back room at the café Nordstrom is tied to a chair. Gemmel opens Nordstrom's bag only to discover a butterfly net and a collection of rocks… not what they were expecting. Gemmel tells them they have to find one of the two Americans, who is clearly the man they're after.

Joel and Hiram are at their hotel getting ready to go out for dinner at the Café of the Seven Lotus Blossoms. Hiram cuts himself whilst shaving so Joel goes to his friend's bag to pull out a styptic pencil however in the bag he discovers a skindiver's outfit and some magnetic bombs. Whilst looking for a small box that he uses to store his styptic pencil Hiram accidentally activates one of the bombs…

Hiram manages to disarm it and realises that he must have picked up the wrong bag at the airport. As they go to take the bombs to the authorities Hiram is again enthusiastically greeted by Natasha in the hotel lobby much to his bemusement. Gemmel, who is watching proceedings from a distance, indicates that she has again got the wrong man and she should be going after Joel. Wang escorts Joel off at gunpoint. Hiram shrugs wistfully and picks up his case. He goes to the café where he checks in the suitcase and sits down to wait for Joel. Joel is in the back room, tied to a chair. Gemmel walks in with Joel's suitcase.

Gemmel slowly opens the case, expecting the worst. But he finds shirts, ties and underwear and angry, tells Wang to go and get the other American, Hiram.

Hiram is busy eating in the café. Natasha sits down with him and eventually persuades him to dance with her. As she manoeuvres him near the drapes, where Wang waits ready to knock him unconscious, Hiram makes a fancy step and another dancer suffers the consequences. This happens again and again until the dance finishes.

Natasha offers to take Hiram to Joel. As they enter the back room he is greeted by Gemmel and Wang. Gemmel decrees that Hiram must be killed and pulls out his knife, Wang produces a sword, Hiram defends himself with his trusty umbrella and manages to escape to the main café where the fight continues. Hiram manages to regain his suitcase whilst keeping Gemmel and Wang at bay.

Joel and Nordstrom are tied up together on the boat. Hiram swims out and places the bombs on to the hull of the boat. Joel and Nordstrom roll off the boat into the water where Hiram helps them get to shore just as the bomb explodes and the ship is destroyed.

Notes:

Just in case you were wondering sea cucumbers are soft-bodied cousins of sea urchins and starfish. Their dried bodies are prized for their medicinal properties and often used as an aphrodisiac.

Total cost of this episode was $39,093.

Anthony Capps, who is credited as staging the dance in this episode, sued Phil Rapp and CNP in October 1956. The essence of his complaint was that he was hired as dance director of 13 films of "Hiram Holliday" but they only used him in this one. Rapp and CNP emphatically denied the existence of any such employment relationship. Copp was claiming damages of around $45k. The suit was settled out of court.

The last version of this script was dated 14th August 1956. Phil Rapp and Dick Powell were working all the hours they could but they still needed help getting the scripts written. A number of other writers were hired but Rapp would not let the scripts go without his input, hence the shared writing credit.

Co-writer John Kohn served as a tail gunner in the US Air Force during World War II. The son of a rabbi he was born in New York in 1925. He graduated with a BA from UCLA and got his first TV credit in 1951 for a contribution to the *Gruen Guild Playhouse*. He wrote for many shows throughout the 1950s but at the end of the decade he moved to London where he started writing for films. From 1979 to 1983 he was the head of production for EMI where he oversaw *The Jazz Singer* amongst other films. He was married to Barbara Jaffe, the daughter of legendary agent and producer Sam Jaffe and died from cancer in March 2002.

The other co-writer Bernard Drew studied film at New York University before moving to the west coast and writing for several early TV shows such as *Lux Video Theatre* and *Douglas Fairbanks Jr Presents*. He returned to New York in 1965 and joined the Gannett newspaper organisation becoming resident film critic until January 1984 when he passed away.

This was the first of three appearances in the show for Sebastian Cabot. Born in London Cabot seemed to specialise in elegant, upper-class and educated roles, yet was born a working class cockney in July 1918..He is perhaps best remembered nowadays for his work with Disney, voicing Bagheera in the 1967 version of *The Jungle Book*, as the narrator of the Winnie the Pooh tales and as the voice of Sir Ector, in *The Sword in the Stone*. But he had a long career in film and TV including playing Porthos in a

1956 TV version of *The Three Musketeers*, and regular roles in shows such as *Checkmate*, *The Beachcomber* and *Family Affair*. He died in August 1977 in Canada,

Mark Dana was born in Detroit, Michigan in June 1920. He had a long career in film and TV from the 1950s through to the 1990s with numerous roles in westerns. A strong actor, with a rich voice and lots of charisma he died in January 2015 at the age of 94.

Although Thurston Hall appears in the credits Prentice does not appear in this episode.

6. The Adventure of the Gibraltar Toad

Script No. 106
Production No. 2605
Sponsored by Jello
Release date: 7th November 1956
BBC first run 10th August 1960 at 18:50, repeated 26th February 1961
Produced, written and directed by Philip Rapp

Cast: Wally Cox (Hiram Holliday), Ainslie Pryor (Joel Smith), Albert Cavens (Gitanillo)

Synopsis:
Wally Cox saves the Rock of Gibraltar from destruction and his own skin at the same time.

Hiram (Cox) goes to Gibraltar in search of a rare type of toad. He is arrested, however, by British authorities who suspect him of being an enemy agent sent to blow up the rock and seal the Mediterranean Sea. A band of gypsies effect his escape, thinking him to be El Gitanillo, their agent sent to explode Gibraltar. When the real Gitanillo (Albert Cavens) arrives at the gypsy camp his identity is questioned. Hiram expertly dancers a flamenco with Carmen (Nephru Malouf), battles El Gitanillo with rapier and dagger to establish himself as the real Gitanillo in order to save the threatened Gibraltar.

BBC Synopsis:
Scotland Yard, gypsies and the British Army are all involved when the invincible Hiram studies the wildlife on the Rock of Gibraltar.

Notes:
What follows is Phil Rapp's original outline for this episode. It was originally called 'The Adventure of the Toads of Gibraltar':

We FADE IN and find JOEL SMITH in the district police headquarters in Madrid. The captain is telling Smith that the Spanish police have apprehended the world's most dangerous man, Hiram Holliday!

Smith is flabbergasted. Where is Hiram? And why is he being held? The captain scoffs at Smith's innocence. You know the man far better than I, says the captain. After all, are you not his accomplice, his confidante? Were you not with him during the affair of the Brittainique, the theft of the Shabandar, etc? Of course, says Joel, but you misunderstand…We misunderstand nothing, says the Captain. The alert Spanish police have apprehended Hiram Holliday in the nick of time or avoid an international disaster; Hiram, they have learned, had planned to blow up the Rock of Gibraltar; Smith reacts, unbelieving and astonished, then suddenly remembers: With a man like Hiram, it could be true! CUT TO a little Spanish town, several miles from Madrid and near Gibraltar. Two gypsy men and a beautiful, scantily clad gypsy girl are standing before an adobe jailhouse, speaking in low tones. We learn from their conversation that Mr Big, the greatest blower-upper of bridges in all Spain, nay all the world, yet unknown by appearance, has been captured before his greatest blast, the Rock itself.

He is being held, in fact, in this very jail, awaiting the arrival of the British and Spanish authorities to transport him to England for deposition and probably execution. They have never met this man, but his accomplishments have preceded him. He is reputed to be suave, dashing, fearless, a great lover, an untouchable athlete etc. It is their duty to effect his release immediately, in order that his most important job might be accomplished! He is part of a gang which wants to blow up the rock.

Inside the jail we find their man: Hiram Holliday. He is conversing with his guard, who has just brought him a plate of Spanish food, which Hiram is savouring with great relish, albeit he has a suggestion or two as to how the tacos might be improved. The guard, a fat, greasy Spaniard, is gloating, between swigs of wine, how he is due a great promotion for his feat. Hiram tells him that he has made a mistake, for Hiram's only interest in Gibraltar is to uncover a rare breed of toad which is known to inhabit the Rock. The guard laughs. Why the blasting powder on Hiram's person? Because the toads are indigenous to deep crevices in the rock and a small amount of the near harmless powder in necessary to dislodge them from their hiding places. As they talk, the girl enters, exuding sex, and lures the tipsy guard away from Hiram while her two confederates, taking the key which she has lifted during a feigned bit of lovemaking with El Gordo, sneak in and release Hiram, spiriting him out a back door. Once away from the jail, the gypsies refuse to permit Hiram to talk until they reach the safety of their caravan, where they rush Hiram into a wagon. Hiram thanks them, but can't understand why they have done it. They smile at each other. He is modest, as advertised. A double-entendre type conversation ensues, and Hiram begins to suspect that they have released the wrong man. Probably, they think he is the man the police think he is.

The girl returns and a scene ensues with her and Hiram. Hiram comes to realise that he is in hot water indeed. The police will never believe his story, so he must remain with the gypsies until the real Mr Big shows up. The caravan comes to a halt and makes camp just outside the town where a bullfight will be held the following day. Singing and dancing begins and Hiram, how dressed as a gypsy, is closely observing the native songs and dances, enjoying himself immensely as is his wont. We now interject a scene showing Joel and the police discovering Hiram's escape and setting out on his trail. As Hiram sits his foot falls asleep, and in an effort to awaken it, he rises and begins to stamp it on the ground. The girl's eyes light as she watches him stamping. A master of the Flamenco. She goes to him and begs for the honor of doing the dance with him. The gypsies move in and watch and Hiram, afraid to refuse upon knowing that Mr Big is known to be a great master of the Flamenco, does the dance to the great delight of the camp,

As he dances a courier runs to one of the gypsy heavies. A message from Mr Big. He has planted the bomb alone and will arrive within the hour. What? The heavies look to Hiram. Could this man be an imposter? (Or they know he is and wish to do away with him quickly). They must find out. They pull Hiram away and confront him. Mr Big is known to have been a great matador. Hiram must prove he is the man by facing a bull.

They spirit a protesting Hiram to the deserted bull ring and loose a ferocious bull, awaiting tomorrow's fight, into the ring. Hiram, armed with only an ill-fitting sport coat and his umbrella, masters the bull and rides triumphantly from the ring on his back. (The police and Joel have finally caught his trail and are present to witness the spectacle). Hiram goes to them and explains. They know, for they have captures the real Mr Big. There is a great problem, however. Mr Big has planted the bomb in the rock, an atomic time bomb with enough force to turn the rock to powder. Mr Big has gloated that the apparatus is set to explode in an hour, and the greatest demolition experts in the world, having gone to the rock and examined the mechanism, have found that the bomb can not only not be dismantled by their skills, for they have never run across such a device, but it cannot even be moved, for the slightest wrong motion will trigger it off. Hiram modestly volunteers to try. He has some experience with explosives and bombs. Willing to try anything, they quickly hustle Hiram to the rock over Joel's protests.

The police and Joel stand on the faraway shore, while Hiram works on the bomb on the rock. A walkie-talkie phone keeps the police in touch with Hiram as he works. The minutes tick by in a tense scene, as zero hour approaches. "I've almost got it," says Hiram. "No, I lost it." This type of dialogue goes back and forth, the reactions of the police and Joel corresponding, when only seconds before zero hour, Hiram triumphantly exclaims that the job is done.

He rejoins the nervously exhausted group who maul him with gratitude for his great abilities in disarming the bomb before the deadline. Hiram reacts. That? It was nothing. I had that fixed in seconds. He holds up a tiny apparatus. Only a matter of fratistating the caniform with the top of my umbrella, he says. They react. Then what was all the confusion? I've got it, I haven't etc.? Oh, says Hiram. This. He holds up a small box and exhibits the contents. The rare Gibraltar toad. "Frisky little fellow. Almost got away," says Hiram moving off and admiring his prize as the police react is disbelief and Joel, calloused by now, shakes his head to camera and deliver his closing remarks.

When it came to the final script there were a few significant changes, predominantly for reasons of budget and to simplify the story:
1. The episode starts with Joel in London, at Scotland Yard. He's left Hiram because he needs to see his dentist in London.
2. The backstory of the toads and the explosive powder disappeared

3. Carmen initially and at some length tried to seduce Hiram. El Gitanillo appears just as they're trying to make Hiram their blood brother. Carmen decides the only way to tell if Hiram is the real Gitanillo is to dance with him. They do, and as far as she is concerned he is genuine and once he's blown up the rock they are to be married.
4. The final decision comes down to a duel, Hiram versus the real El Gitanillo with rapier and dagger. Hiram wins the sword fight. The real El Gitanillo has already planted the explosives in the rock and offers to show them.
5. Joel and the Scotland Yard men have flown down to Gibraltar. Hiram walks into their meeting with the local police and tells all; the local police have captured the gypsies but the bomb has already been planted.
6. The final scene with Hiram disarming the bomb remains relatively intact, though Hiram does indeed come out with the Gibraltar firetoad.

Total cost of this episode was $36,768

7. **The Adventure of the Monaco Hermit Crab**
Script No. 109
Production No. 2607
Sponsored by Sanka
Release date: 14th November 1956
BBC first run 18th August 1960 at 18:50, repeated 18th July 1961
Written by Phillip Rapp

Cast: Wally Cox (Hiram Holliday), Ainslie Pryor (Joel Smith), John Banner (Count Courtebiche), Stanley Adams, (Garreaux), Eva Ralph (Giselle)

Synopsis:
Hiram executes the "Spectre of the Rose" ballet and blithely breaks the bank at Monte Carlo while foiling a ploy to destroy America's economy in "The Monaco Hermit Crab".

While in Monaco to study the migration of the Mediterranean hermit crab, Hiram (Wally Cox) wins at roulette and gains title to a luxury yacht from an unlucky gambler. This involves him in a plot to flood the US with counterfeit money designed to destroy the national economy, for it was planned to smuggle the phony currency into America on the yacht. The plotters try to get Hiram out of the way using a pretty ballet dancer, Giselle (Eva Ralph) as decoy in vain.

Notes:
The final script revision for this episode was done on 14 August 1956. Total cost of this episode was $38,171.

John Banner was born in Austria in January 1910 and studied law at the University of Vienna however he opted to become an actor instead of a lawyer. He was forced to flee his homeland at the age of 28 when Hitler annexed Austria to Nazi Germany. Banner, a Jew, was performing in Switzerland at the time and unable to return to Austria, emigrated to the United States as a political refugee. He had some early success and secured a small number of roles on Broadway but his career was interrupted in 1942 when he became a supply sergeant in the US Army Air Force, which he served until the end of the role. He resumed his acting career once demobbed securing roles in shows such as *The Adventures of Superman*, *The Lone Ranger*, *The Lucy Show*, *The Man From UNCLE* and *Alias Smith and Jones*. His last role was in 1972 after which he retired to Europe, however, just a year later he died form an abdominal haemorrhage in Vienna.

8. **The Adventure of the Hawaiian Hamzah**
Script No. 110
Production No. 2608
Sponsored by Jello
Release date: 21st November 1956
BBC first run 15th August 1960 at 18:50, repeated 12th March 1961
Produced, written and directed by Philip Rapp

Cast: Wally Cox (Hiram Holliday), Ainslie Pryor (Joel Smith), John Wengraf, Lei Aloha, Al Cavens, Thurston Hall (Prentice), Russell Hicks, Jonathan Hole, Russ Thorson, Paul Wexler

Story:
Joel and Hiram are in the Royal Hawaiian Lanai and Surf Bar in Waikiki. Hiram is

reading a book by Professor Henry P Codd on the language of the islands. The author has been helping Hiram in his search for "the elusive hamzah...a language sign representing the Hawaiian lost consonant..."

They've been in Hawaii a week and Joel is getting frustrated by Hiram's lack of action. Hiram leaves to go and have lunch with Professor Codd. But as Hiram leaves Prentice walks in. He's in Hawaii to cover the signing of the Pacific Mutual Assistance Pact at Pearl Harbour tomorrow. Prentice chews Joel out for living on expenses and not doing his job, and tells him that he's sending him back to the States.

Hiram returns from his lunch just as Joel is checking out. As Hiram is talking to Joel he is bumped slightly by a portly man with a beard, it is Gemmel, thinly disguised with an eye patch. Hiram doesn't quite recognise him.

Gemmel, along with another man and a woman, Moana, get into the lift. They go up to a room where a thin, gaunt man lets them in. The man gets a small box out of the safe and hands it to Gemmel who feverishly unwraps it. It is an elaborately carved pen, about a foot long. He explains to Moana that this turns sea water to ice. He demonstrates it on a glass of water.

The plan is for Moana to give the pen to the American envoy tomorrow who will sign the treaty with it and then toss it into Pearl Harbor, imprisoning the American fleet.

Joel and Hiram are in the restaurant eating, watching Prentice buttering up the diplomat Duncan over their meal. Duncan tells Prentice he is apparently to be presented with a ceremonial pen this evening. Although there are rumors a foreign power may try and block the signing Duncan is confident things will go ahead as planned.

Moana comes on as part of the entertainment for the evening and everyone is distracted by her dancing. As she finishes Keoki enters, carrying the box with the pen in on the flat of his sword. Duncan rises and starts forward for the presentation.

The small Asiatic man opens the switch box and pulls the main switch. The lights go out. Gunfire ensues. The lights come back on.

The Asian man has been shot and dropped the pen. Hiram picks it up. Gemmel sees that Hiram has picked it up and send Moana to get it from him, for Holliday, he says, has an Achilles heel—women.

Hiram goes to see her, but gives Joel the pen, just to be on the safe side. As Hiram makes his way behind the stage 'the dance of the spears' is announced as another part of the evening's entertainment. Gemmel doesn't believe that Hiram doesn't have the pen so orders his henchman to strip Holliday.

Hiram grabs a spear and knocks the gun out of Gemmel's hand. The henchman grabs the other spear and starts battling Hiram. The fight spills into the restaurant where the patrons believe it to be part of the entertainment.

In their hotel room the morning after the fight Gemmel, Keoki and Moana try to figure out how to get the pen. Gemmel decides to let the police do it for them; he has sent Hiram a secret document, a map of the Pearl Harbour minefields. He has also told the police that Hiram's got it, so once they arrest Hiram they'll simply go to his room and pick up the pen.

Hiram and Joel are having breakfast but Hiram is still mystified by the significance of the pen. Prentice interrupts their breakfast. Hiram, playing with the pen, discovers it doesn't write very well so decides to moisten it using a nearby fishbowl.

Hiram goes off to try and save the newly frozen fish. A messenger appears at the table with a packet for Hiram. Prentice snatches it from Joel only for two publishers to follow up the messenger and arrest Prentice.

Moana and Keoki are tossing Hiram's room looking for the pen. Keoki hides in the wardrobe when Hiram enters the room, whilst Moana offers Hiram a free hula lesson. In the course of the conversation Keoki sneak out of the wardrobe and knocks Hiram unconscious.

Later on, Joel makes his way to Hiram's room to discover Hiram sitting on the floor recovering, Moana, Keoki and the pen having disappeared.

With only an hour to the signing Hiram decides they have to get out to the aircraft carrier where it is taking place. Hiram and Joel 'borrow' a plane from the airbase to get out to the carrier

Hiram is flying the plane and contacts the aircraft carrier in the hopes of landing. Duncan recognises the name so persuades the captain to give Hiram permission to land. With the use of some stock footage Hiram crashes the plane over the side of the carrier. A sodden Hiram and Joel are rescued by the crew and brought aboard. Just as they are about to be clapped in irons Hiram borrows the pen from Duncan and demonstrates its power.

Later, over drinks Prentice is frustrated. No one will tell him anything and the government have practically ordered him to keep Joel and Hiram doing what they're doing…

Notes:

Total cost of this episode was $40,325.

John Wengraf, another Austrian actor, was born in April 1897. He was a matinee idol in Europe throughout the 1920s and well into the following decade however as the Nazis rose to power he emigrated to Britain in 1933. His stage career flourished and he appeared in many early BBC TV shows but in 1941 he made his Broadway debut alongside Helen Hayes in *Candle in the Wind* and he opted to stay in the USA.

After meeting Hiram he appeared in a number of TV shows including *The Untouchables*, *The Man From UNCLE* and *The Time Tunnel*. He retired in 1966 and died eleven years later.

Hiram can always find a weapon to hand, even if it's not his trusty umbrella

9. **The Adventure of the Swiss Titmouse**
Script No. 108
Production No. 2611
Sponsored by Sanka
Release date: 28th November 1956
BBC first run 16th August 1960 at 18:50, repeated 4th June 1961
Written by Phillip Rapp and Robert Riley Crutcher
Directed by William J. Hole Jr.

Cast: Wally Cox (Hiram Holliday), Ainslie Pryor (Joel Smith), Rene Korper (King), Violet Rensing (Princess), Thurston Hall (Prentice).

Synopsis:
A plot against a child monarch is foiled by the hero of The Adventures of Hiram Holliday

Hiram (Wally Cox), while in Switzerland to record the mating call of the Swiss Titmouse, inadvertently learns that the visiting young ruler's life is in danger. In his plan to help the boy (Rene Korper) and his princess aunt (Violet Rensing), Hiram disguises himself as a scarecrow in a Swiss meadow and later engages in a thrilling fight on a cable car high over the Swiss valleys.

Story:
Hiram and Joel are in Switzerland where Joel is meeting Prentice as he comes off a train. The paper has been promising its readers details of Hiram's latest adventure for the last three weeks but Joel has not submitted any stories. Prentice has come out to see what is going on.

Spying that they are Americans the station master asks Joel and Prentice if they have an American flag for he wants to fly it alongside the Swiss flag in honor of Hiram Holliday. Joel and Prentice are perplexed. It seems that every road and mountain pass leading into Switzerland has been heavily mined with dynamite, intended to blow up the mountains and crush any invaders. However, a landslide set off the firing mechanism which Hiram calmly defused, using just a picnic fork.

In their hotel Hiram is listening to a tape recorder. Prentice is convinced that secret agents are everywhere, and Hiram has sniffed them out. But as they enter Hiram's room, seeing Hiram dressed in lederhosen, they discover that he was listening to the mating call of the yellow breasted Swiss titmouse. A horn sounds—a signal for Hiram that the titmouse he was watching has returned to the nest but Prentice is convinced he's off on his next great adventure.

Hiram, dressed as a scarecrow, is standing in a meadow. As he studies the bird we see a small boy, Peter, come up a nearby incline; he is about eight years old, looking like he's escaped from Eton, very regal. He calls to his Aunt Heidi in German. It's clear they are being chased by someone. Hiram watches them.

Heidi joins Peter. She's a blonde teenager with warm blue eyes, wearing a trench coat, carrying a bundle of clothes and looking frightened. They're trying to get to the border but Heidi thinks their only chance is to change their clothes and blend in with the people in the village. They change near Hiram, who is still posing as a scarecrow.

As they emerge in their new outfits, Konrad, Robert and Chernik arrive and try to grab them but Hiram comes to their rescue with the aid of his umbrella.

Hiram strips off his scarecrow outfit and accompanies Peter and Heidi on their way, As they talk Hiram discovers that it is in fact King Peter and Princess Heidi who are with him; they were kidnapped from their country and are being chased by Count Chernik and his men. Hiram suggests they go back to the inn.

As the bad guys recover, they look at Hiram's umbrella which has his name on and conclude they've probably headed to the inn.

At the inn Prentice and Joel are finishing up dinner but they go to their room just before Hiram and his new friends arrive. Hiram books Heidi and Peter into a room but the hotel clerk is not to be trusted and once they've checked in, tells someone they've arrived.

Heidi and Peter's room is in the same corridor as Joel's and when Joel sees Hiram with Heidi he rushes in to grab Mr Prentice but by the time he grabs him, Hiram and his friends have disappeared and Prentice is convinced Joel is seeing things.

Hiram, Heidi and Peter are welcomed into their room by Robert, Konrad and Chernik and held at gunpoint when Prentice knocks on the door, determined to show Joel that he was seeing things. Chernik stays in the doorway and denies knowing Hiram or the girl Joel alleges he brought into the room.

Chernik tells Robert to take Hiram out on the slope and arrange for him to have an accident. But before he leaves Hiram admires a bust of Napoleon that Chernik himself made. Hiram admires the artist's style but says he can do better. Chernik, with the traditional ego of an evil guy, gets him to demonstrate.

Chernik is astounded by his talents. Hiram grabs his umbrella as if to leave but Chernik stops him. Hiram opens his umbrella as Konrad and Robert fire at him. The bad guys are astounded as the bullets end up on the floor as twisted chunks of metal. Hiram, Heidi and Peter hurriedly leave.

Chernik and his men give chase but Hiram, Heidi and Peter merge into a group of yodellers who are in the common room of the hotel. Joel hears Hiram yodelling and helps distract one of the bad guys so the trio can leave the inn.

Soon Heidi, Hiram and Peter are working their way along a narrow pass on the side of a snow-covered mountain trying to make their way to a cable car with Chernik, Robert and Konrad giving chase. The cable car will get them over the border to safety however they discover it is out of order. Hiram manages to fix it—with a roll of friction tape and a hairpin no less—but as they get into the car Chernik and his men arrive. A fight ensures which Hiram, with the aid of his trusty umbrella, eventually wins.

Joel and Prentice are still watching the scarecrow, unaware that it's been replaced by a real one. When an avalanche wipes out the scarecrow, they are distraught...until Hiram arrives in their room along with a recording of the mating call of the Swiss Titmouse.

Notes:
Total cost of this episode was $43,867.
The Hollywood Reporter[34] enjoyed this episode:

"Producer-writer Phil Rapp's hunch that Paul Gallico's character, Hiram Holliday, who excels in every sport, is a mental wizard and accomplishes acts of derring-do against impossible odds, could only have been played by the self-effacing, innocuous looking Wally Cox, still pays off with high laugh returns. In this episode Holliday starts off by saving Switzerland from a catastrophic dynamite explosion by dismembering the initial charge, engages in deft swordplay with his umbrella, proves artistic prowess by sculpting an artistic bust of Caesar in two minutes,

---

34 30 November 1956

and winds up by saving a young monarch and his sister from villainous politicians as he hangs from a cable car traversing the Alps.

In his first directorial effort William J Hole accomplished something we've been advising veteran directors to do for some time, namely using tight close-ups on faces when dialogue takes the place of action. It calls for more work on the directorial chore but pays off with more viewer interest, as witness the successful use of ECUs on the *Dragnet* show. Ably foiling for Cox were regulars Thurston Hall as his blustering publisher and Ainslie Prior, a promising comic in his own right, whose weakness for food (a clever side touch) keeps him unaware of the Holliday deeds he should be reporting to his paper. Effectively good were Ivan Triesault as the villain, Rene Karper as the young monarch and Violet Rensing as his sister. Oh yes, Cox did a bang up job of yodelling too."

This was indeed William J Hole's first job as director. A Los Angeles native he was born in December 1918 and worked in various roles in the industry before becoming a director. After working with Hiram he continued to direct, right up until his last credit, the 1970s series *The Bionic Woman*, although his longest job was as an associate producer on the now almost legendary soap opera *Peyton Place*, which he worked on for four hundred and forty nine episodes throughout the 1960s. He died in February 1990.

Heidi, who in the scripts is described as "can't be much more than eighteen or nineteen", was played by Violet Rensing, a German actress who was born in July 1927 in Berlin, making her substantially more than eighteen or nineteen. She was named a Wampas Baby Star alongside Lita Milan in 1956 and this helped her towards a career with roles in shows such as *The Third Man* and *One Step Beyond*. She died in 2011 in Los Angeles. She had one son, Rene Korper, who was born in Germany on 14 April, 1948 and who plays Peter in this episode. He had a short career as an actor starring in a handful of TV shows such as *The Loretta Young Show* and *Death Valley Days* before leaving the industry at age 15.

10. The Adventure of the Wrong Rembrandt

Script No. 113
Production No. 2612
Sponsored by Jello
Release date: 5th December 1956
BBC first run 17th August 1960 at 18:50, repeated 26th March 1961
Written, produced and directed by Phillip Rapp

Cast: Wally Cox (Hiram Holliday), Ainslie Pryor (Joel Smith), Jacques Aubuchon (Carlos), Josanne Mariani (Cathy), J Pat O'Malley (Jennings), Louis Mercier (Inspector Gilbert), Fred Cavens (Inspector Ducasse)

Synopsis:
Adding to his already extensive list of skills, Hiram Holliday (Wally Cox) demonstrates his great artistry as a painter in "The Wrong Rembrandt".

Solely for his amusement Hiram becomes adept at duplicating art treasures. The hobby spells trouble for the talented globetrotter and his reporter-friend, Joel Smith

(Ainslie Pryor) when the two are in Paris during the theft of a valuable painting from the Louvre.

Jossanne Mariani, French beauty, appears in this episode.

Story:
Joel is at the Police Prefecture in (presumably) Paris denying he has any connection to a robbery at the Louvre. Somebody has stolen a collection of masterpieces from the museum…and since they found a Rembrandt in his hotel room, Inspector Ducasse thinks Joel is one of the criminals. But Joel says it is a copy, painted by his friend Hiram Holliday. The police are waiting for a director of the Louvre to verify the Rembrandt and then they will arrest Joel.

But the phone rings and the director informs Ducasse that he thinks it's a copy. Just as Joel is about to walk out Ducasse received another phone call. Another director of the Louvre believes the Rembrandt to be genuine. Ducasse lets Joel, however, and once he's gone, gives orders for him to be followed, so they can find the rest of the paintings.

Hiram and Joel are on a train, that unsurprisingly looks just like the one that took them up to Scotland in the second episode. and as they settle into the compartment Hiram explains to Joel that he took up copying masterpieces just to see if he could do it. As they talk Joel recognises a man walking by the compartment—it's Inspector Gilbert from the Surete. He's being followed!

Hiram's pigeon Homer is also on the train, in the baggage compartment. Hiram is about to check on him but Carlos walks into their compartment, claiming it as his own. Hiram apologises and they leave. As Carlos, Jennings and Cathy settle into the compartment, Jennings the very English butler reveals that they orchestrated the theft. Jennings' master, Lord Windemere, is to be buried in Westminster Abbey however they've put the paintings in the coffin and when the furore has died down, they'll recover them. Their contact in Paris will dispose of the Lord's body.

Whilst Jennings goes to check on the coffin in the baggage car Carlos and Cathy discover Hiram's copy of the Rembrandt which they left on the luggage shelf when they changed compartment, but of course the criminal duo think it's genuine. Hiram comes back to get his painting and after some disagreement Carlos, still thinking it's genuine and Hiram's an oddball, lets him have it.

Joel and Inspector Gilbert are in the dining car. Hiram explains the situation to

Gilbert but he's not interested. Hiram goes to check on his pigeon and meets Jennings in the baggage car. After he's fed the bird he leaves, only to be met by Carlos and Cathy who are going to see Jennings. Hiram goes back to his seat whilst Carlos, fearful that more paintings will be taken from the coffin, checks the box only to discover the Rembrandt in it. He believes Hiram must have returned it to the coffin right under the nose of the butler!

Carlos send Cathy to see Hiram, who's in his compartment admiring the copy of the Rembrandt. Cathy, still thinking of Hiram as a master criminal, tries to seduce him. Carlos and Jennings discover the situation, although Cathy tells him Hiram forced himself on her, and Carlos declares he will kill Hiram as a crime of passion. But he hasn't the time to kill him with a gun, so shows Hiram his umbrella, which is just like Hiram's although, being a bad guy, the tip of his is impregnated with a poison. Hiram, suggesting he may well have swapped umbrellas, makes his escape.

Hiram goes back to see Gilbert who is still in the dining car. Cathy overhears his declaration that he still thinks Joel stole the masterpieces. Cathy goes back to see Carlos and tells him they've been after the wrong man. Joel is the one they want!

As Joel makes his way back to his compartment Carlos knocks him unconscious. Inspector Gilbert discovers them and Carlos tells him that Joel had a bad fall, however he is a doctor and will look after him. Meanwhile Jennings catches up with Hiram in the baggage compartment and knocks him unconscious. He puts Hiram's Rembrandt in the coffin.

On the Channel boat the guard discovers and wakes up Hiram. The guard tells him to see a doctor. Perhaps the same one who is seeing to his friend Joel. In the boat's operating theatre Carlos is about to stab Joel when Hiram enters. A fight ensues, with Jennings using an umbrella and Hiram using surgical instruments (just for a change!). Hiram knocks out Jennings and Carlos just as Gilbert arrives and Joel wakes up.

Notes:
Total cost of this episode was $33,006.

The marvellous Jacques Aubuchon who played Carlos in this episode was born in Fitchburg, Massachusetts in October 1924. He served as an interpreter in the military during WWII and after the war studied at the American Theater Wing for Advance Studies. In 1949 he made his Broadway debut, starring in *The Madwoman of Chaillot* and his TV debut in a show called *Café de Paris* for the DuMont Network. He never looked back, going on to make over three hundred television appearances, more than two dozen films and hundreds of TV commercials. The father of writer and producer Remi Aubuchon (*24*, *Falling Skies*, *Stargate Universe*) he died at the age of 67 in December 1991 from a heart attack.

James Patrick Francis O'Malley, to give him his full name, was born to an Irish family in Burnley, Lancashire, England in March 1904. He started his career in the mid-1920s as a music hall singer and by 1930 he had become the lead singer for the Jack Hylton Orchestra. The Orchestra toured the USA in 1936 but when it came time to return to the UK O'Malley opted to stay in the USA. He found work in radio as an actor and eventually decamped to Hollywood to try his luck in the movies. His first role was in the unremarkable 1940 film *Captain Caution* which starred Victor Mature but further work soon followed. He spent a year on Broadway in the mid-1940s starring in an adaptation of Agatha Christie's *And Then There Were None* but soon returned to the west coast, and his TV career soon blossomed with guest roles in many shows of the time. He went on to appear in over a hundred different TV series across his thirty-two-year TV career. He died from heart disease in California in February 1985.

11. **THE ADVENTURE OF THE DANCING MOUSE**
Script No. 107
Production No. 2609
Sponsored by Sanka
Release date: 12th December 1956
BBC first run 11th August 1960 at 18:50, repeated 5th March 1961
Directed by George M Cahan
Written and produced by Philip Rapp

Cast: Wally Cox (Hiram Holliday), Ainslie Pryor (Joel Smith), Leon Askin (Drago), Ziva Shapir (Marlene), Ida Moore (Mrs Huckaby), Thurston Hall (Harrison Prentice), Tony Eustrel (Alexander), Thor Johnson (Bandini), Tony George (Italian Policeman), William Justine (Police Sergeant), Roger Til (High Dive Barker)

Synopsis:
With a camera of his own design Hiram Holliday (Wally Cox) inadvertently snaps a picture of two revolutionary leaders who pursue him with deadly intent. The chase

takes Hiram and his pursuers through an entire Italian carnival, where he is carted off in a phone booth by the carnival strongman (Tor Johnson), is kissed in the Tunnel of Love by Ziva Shapir (Miss Israel) and makes a 125 foot dive into three feet of water.

Summary:
Prentice is not happy. He places a phone call to Smith in Genoa, Italy and chews him out about making up stories; Hiram Holliday blowing up the rock of Gibraltar, engaged to a gypsy, fighting a duel with a dagger and a rapier. Although Smith defends himself Prentice doesn't listen and for the sake of peace and quiet Smith acquiesces. Prentice tells him not to submit another story unless it includes proof—pictures.

Hiram tells Smith he's going on a nature hunt but Smith turns down his invitation to join him.

Hiram is sneaking around a carnival ground looking for wildlife with his camera. He sneaks into a tent and takes a picture of a couple of suspicious looking characters, Alexander and Drago. Whilst the former flees, Hiram tries to persuade the latter that he was actually in pursuit of the Japanese dancing mouse but Drago tells Hiram to hand over the picture he took, otherwise Hiram will not leave the tent alive. When Bandini, a wrestler goon enters the tent looking to make good on the threat, Hiram hands over the camera and flees. Bandini destroys the camera. Drago figures Hiram must have the photo and tells him to give chase.

Drago catches up with Alexander who's in another tent, this one also has a harem girl, Marlene, putting on her make-up. After an argument Marlene tells the men not to worry, she will find Hiram or rather Hiram will find Marlene…

As Hiram makes his way through the carnival he comes across an empty phone booth however an old lady, Mrs Huckaby, stops him from using it as she's waiting for a call about her sunglasses that she's lost. Spying Bandini catching him up Hiram manages to distract Mrs Huckaby and call Smith. He regales him with tales of his adventure only to be interrupted by Mrs Huckaby, who's still waiting for her call. Mild mannered Hiram hangs up on Smith. Smith calls the police.

Bandini catches up with Hiram and escorts him into Marlene's tent but Hiram manages to give the photo to Mrs Huckaby, telling her it's a postcard that needs mailing.

Hiram thought Marlene had been locked up in Paris but it seems he ate the evidence. Drago wants the picture but Marlene persuades him that she should take

Hiram into the Tunnel of Love where she will be "most persuasive", however Bandini and Drago will act as chaperones.

Smith and a policeman have arrived at the carnival but cannot find Hiram, however Mrs Huckaby buttonholes the policeman to help look for her sunglasses. The discussion is interrupted when Hiram and Marlene emerge from the Tunnel of Love with Marlene enthusiastically kissing Hiram. The policeman concludes Hiram really isn't in much trouble at all and hauls Smith off to the police station to have a word about wasting police time.

Hiram manages to escape Marlene's clutches and phones Smith at the police station. He's identified one of the men in the photo as Alexander, the former dictator of Bulgaria. But Alexander is supposedly in Paris and not meant to be allowed out of France…

Smith manages to persuade the Italian police to call the police in Paris. The Paris police however say Alexander has not left the country. Smith makes his way back to the carnival as Bandini catches up with Hiram.

Hiram escapes and shows off his shooting skills at the shooting gallery just as Drago and Bandini arrive. Hiram again escapes and makes his way to Marlene's tent. She tells him to hide in the dressing room of another performer who as it happens won't be in tonight. That performer would have been diving from a 120 ft high tower into a 5 ft deep tank of water.

Hiram takes his place and Smith and the police arrive just in time to watch his dive. Drago meanwhile takes a gun from the shooting gallery and starts taking potshots at Hiram. Everyone watches as Hiram makes his dive

Hiram emerges from the pool and is greeted by Smith and the police. However, it seems that Mrs Huckaby mailed the 'post card' to her nephew in Des Moines. Smith submits his story but of course he has no proof…

Notes:
Total cost of this episode was $35,593.

Phil Rapp had a problem. The show was his baby and although he had help in writing the scripts he was finding himself stuck in the edit suite more than he bargained for.

To help ease the demands on his time George M Cahan stepped in to direct this episode. Cahan was an executive producer at California National Productions. Having directed numerous episodes of *The Cisco Kid* and *Boston Blackie* he was a reliable pair of hands, mid-way through a three-year contract with CNP--after which he formed his own production company and returned to directing. He died in 1991 from pneumonia.

This episode, which was filmed in September that year, saw the TV debut of Israeli actress Ziva Shapir. Shapir was born Ziva Blechman in Haifa, Israel in March 1933. She moved to the United States at age 15 when she was sent to live with her aunt and uncle in St Louis, Missouri. After graduation she returned to Israel where she studied acting and served a two-year stint in the Israeli army. In 1954 she was named Queen of the Wine Festival and was rewarded with a six-week trip to the United States. That same year she made three films in Israel and again travelled to New York, where she was spotted by Universal talent scout Maurice Bergman. Under long term contract to Universal she made numerous films and had guest roles in TV shows such as *Perry Mason*, *The Man From UNCLE* and *Batman*. She returned to Israel in the late 1960s and eventually retired.

12. **The Adventure of the Christmas Fruchtbrod**
Script No. 112
Production No. 2613
Sponsored by Jello
Release date: 19th December 1956
BBC first run 22nd December 1960 at 19:05
Written by Phillip Rapp and Robert Riley Crutcher

Cast: Wally Cox (Hiram Holliday), Ainslie Pryor (Joel Smith), Rene Korper (King Peter), Violet Rensing (Princess Heidi), Greta Thyssen (Frieda)

Synopsis:
Globe-trotting Hiram Holliday (Wally Cox) and his reporter friend Joel Smith (Ainslie Pryor) spend Christmas Eve in Vienna preparing for the traditional Austrian Yule dinner when trouble strikes.

The troubles come on the wings of Hiram's homing pigeon "Homer", which carries a message that young King Peter (Rene Korper) is being held captive in a nearby tavern. Hiram rescues the king and his princess-aunt (Violet Rensing) after a hilarious fight among the beer kegs of the Hofbrau and an inspired duel. Greta Thyssen, the former "Miss Denmark", portrays the innkeeper's niece.

BBC Synopsis:
In Vienna Hiram meets Princess Heidi again and once more his friend Joel is distracted from his favourite pastime of chasing food.

Notes:
Many sources refer to this episode as 'The Adventure of the Christmas Fruchtbrod Day'. Fruchtbrod is an anglicised version of Früchtebrot, a Christmas cake made with dark bread, nuts and dried fruit that is particularly common in the southern Germany and Spline region. Unfortunately, neither the script nor an English language version of this episode is currently available.

This was Robert Riley Crutcher's second and final contribution to the adventures of Hiram Holliday. He was born in August 1911 in St Louis, Missouri and started his writing career, as did so many, working for radio in the 1930s and 40s. He was one of the main writers on *The Eddie Bracken Show* and created *The Fabulous Doctor Tweedy*. He dabbled in film but broke through with the advent of television in the following decade. It was his work on *Topper*, where he met Phil Rapp, that got him the job on this show after which he went on to write for shows such as *The Thin Man* and *Bewitched*. He died on 10 August, 1974 aged just 62 and is buried in the Hollywood Memorial Cemetery.

13. The Adventure of the Romantic Pigeon

Script No. 111
Production No. 2610
Sponsored by Sanka
Release date: 26th December 1956
BBC first run 19th August 1960 at 18:50

Produced and directed by Philip Rapp
Written by Doris Gilbert and Philip Rapp
Associate Producer: Robert Stillman

Cast: Wally Cox (Hiram Holliday), Ainslie Pryor (Joel Smith), Robert H Harris (Swammerdam), Hollis Irving (Greta), Karl Lindt (Van Hooten), Thurston Hall (Prentice), Paul Newlan (Holbein), Fred Cavens (Conductor), Al Cavens (Franz)

Story:
Hiram and Joel are in Amsterdam. Joel is on the phone to Mr Prentice who is unhappy to hear that Hiram is writing an article on pigeons. Prentice tells Joel he wants him to interview Henry Van Houten "the world's greatest authority on nuclear fusion", who is travelling from Amsterdam tonight on his way to New York. Van Houten has "an atomic formula that will light up the whole world" and is going to present it to the United Nations. As Joel tries to explain things to Hiram, Hiram is distracted by the return of Homer, the pigeon…

Hiram has been training Homer, sending him out with a message attached to his leg "usually some poetry of my own composition". Homer returns bearing a bit of "rather unbridled Keats written in a feminine hand."

Hiram brings the bird on the train to Rotterdam. Hiram and Joel start looking for Van Houten, as do a couple of Germans, Swammerdam and Franz, who plan to make him an offer he can't refuse. The ticket inspector comes to check Joel and Hiram's tickets and although Hiram tries to hide Homer, the bird escapes. Joel heads for the dining car, missing Swammerdam and Franz who come upon Hiram sitting alone, and think he is Van Houten. Hiram solves the mathematical problem they set him and they offer him a blank cheque for his "little secret". Hiram, thinking they mean Homer, declines their offer. Swammerdam offers Hiram over a million dollars for 'Homer'; he ups the offer to four million bur Hiram still declines.

Franz holds Hiram at knifepoint as Joel returns. Joel found Homer, or perhaps it was vice versa as the pigeon flew into Joel's soup in the dining car. Swammerdam and Franz realise they were about to make a horrendous mistake and leave.

Hiram notices a message strapped to Homer's leg—it's poetry by Shelley. Joel and Hiram—finally—set about looking for Van Houten. Hiram wanders into the dining car and accidentally knocks a lady's drink over. As he sits down to talk to her Homer appears, however Greta, the lady is just as excited to see him as Hiram, for the pigeon brings her a message. She reads the quote from Shelley and waxes lyrical to Hiram about her mystery man "tall, with a bronzed brow…his shoulders are broad, he moves like a panther…his gaze is keen and questing…"

She departs to send more poetry via Hiram. As she leaves Joel appears, he's had no luck finding Van Houten and the guard, annoyed by them keeping the pigeon in the dining car, says he will throw them off the train at the next stop.

Swammerdam and Franz have however found Van Houten in his compartment, just as Greta, the daughter, returns. Swammerdam has arranged for them all to leave the train at the next stop.

At the next stop Hiram and Joel are sitting somewhat morosely on the platform as they spy Greta, her father, Swammerdam and Franz leaving. Joel recognises them as the men who are after Van Houten. Joel goes to phone the police as Hiram hitches a ride on the back of their car.

In a barn at Holbein's farm Van Houten is forced to hand over his secret—or see his daughter killed. Hiram enters and using the distraction Greta ties the formula to Home, breaks a window and sets the bird free so that he will return to his owner. A moment later and Homer is back, having returned to Hiram – Greta is amazed. Swammerdam holds them at gunpoint whilst Franz takes the bird and recovers the formula.

A fight ensues which Hiram, with the aid of his trust umbrella, wins.

Back in their hotel room Prentice phones Joel, picking holes in the story he filed.

Notes:

Total cost of this episode was $36,751.

An opening scene was written and subsequently discarded whereby Prentice is a little more favourable towards Joel and Hiram:

FADE IN:
EXT. NEW YORK CITY – DAY – FULL SHOT
DISSOLVE:
INT. PRENTICE'S OFFICE – DAY

Prentice, at his desk, beaming over some copy sheets. A shirtsleeved proofreader, complete with green visor, stands beside him.

PRENTICE
(chuckling)
Capital! Fine circulation booster! Two-dimensional. Gets the kids out and the

grown-ups, too.
The Adventures of Hiram Holliday.

PROOFREADER
Is that stuff really on the level, Mr Prentice?

PRENTICE
On the level! This Holliday's the most gifted man in the world! A knight of the Round Table! Born five hundred years too late. Make the banner eighty-eight-point Gothic and start the series in our next Sunday Supplement.

PROOFREADER
Yes sir.

PRENTICE
(points to cut)
Look at that! The Adventure of the Attache Case. Captured a gang of spies, recovered a diplomatic pouch and tamed a ferocious lion.

The CAMERA has been moving in on the picture of Hiram and the lion. The still goes into action. A MONTAGE follows with Prentice's VOICE over as the story changes. He reads the following titles.

PRENTICE'S VOICE (o.s)
The Adventure of the False Monarch
The Adventure of the Hollow Umbrella
The Adventure of the Sea Cucumber

And whatever other flashbacks are shown
BACK TO SCENE

PRENTICE
This can go on forever my boy. Right now Holliday and Joel Smith are in Amsterdam on the trail of the world's most famous atomic scientist – Van Hooten. I

can just see the story as Hiram—

PROOFREADER
Mr Prentice – I don't think Smith got your cable about Van Hooten. He wired Holliday's working on the life and habits of the homing pigeon.

PRENTICE
Yes. Well, that's just the boy's way of—
(bombshell)
Homing pigeon! Hand me that phone

Co-writer Doris Gilbert came to the show having written a handful of films but having already made the breakthrough to television. She was the daughter of Russian born composer L Wolfe Gilbert and his wife and was born in New York in 1914. At the age of twenty she started writing for World Broadcasting in New York but by 1937 had gone to the west coast intent on becoming a screenwriter. During the 1940s she started writing for Republic Studios eventually moving into television and writing for shows such as *The Adventures of Superman*, *Mr and Mrs North* and *Science Fiction Theatre*. She died in December 1993.

14. **The Adventure of the Sturmzig Cuneiform**
Script No. 115
Production No. 2614
Sponsored by Jello
Release date: 2nd January 1957
BBC first run 12th August 1960 at 18:50, repeated 19th July 1961
Written by Richard M. Powell
Directed by William J Hole Jr.

Cast: Wally Cox (Hiram), Ainslie Pryor (Jorl Smith), Thurston Hall, Hillevi Rombin, Kenneth Alton, Harold Dyrenforth, Kurt Katch

Synopsis:

Hiram Holliday (Wally Cox) runs great risk to acquire clay tablets with cuneiform writing in the small monarchy of Sturmzig. Hillevi Rombin (Miss Universe of 1955) makes her television debut as a dramatic actress in the episode, playing opposite Hiram as the young Queen of Sturmzig. Hiram finally obtains the sturmzig clay tablets – with their information about the Assyrian Onion Market of 2301 BC – only after escaping from a dungeon and fighting two skilled swordsmen.

Notes:

Frustratingly this is another of those episodes for which no script exists in the archives and no English language version of the programme can be found.

Swedish actress Hillevi Rombin did indeed win the Miss Universe beauty pageant in 1955 but there was much more to her than that. Prior to entering the competition she was the Swedish national decathlon champion with track and field, downhill skiing and gymnastics beign her forte. Part of her prize for winning the beauty pageant was a one-year contract with Universal Pictures and she moved to Hollywood for a year where she studied acting alongside Clint Eastwood and Barbara Eden amongst others. Whilst travelling around the USA she met and married G David Schine, whose family was in the hotel business. She retired from acting to focus on married life. They had six children together and their marriage lasted just under forty years. Sadly both she, her husband and one of their sons died in a plane crash in 1996. She was sixty-two.

Kurt Katch was born Isser Kac in Grodno, Poland in January 1893. He was a veteran of the German and Austrian theatre, including Max Reinhardt's School of Drama in Berlin. During WWI he was a prisoner of war in Germany but he escaped imprisonment in WWII by fleeing to the United States in 1938 where he established himself as an actor. He appeared in films such as *The Mask of Dimitrious* and *The Strange Death of Adolf Hitler* and had a long career in TV guesting in many shows throughout the 1950s including *Space Patrol* and *The Adventures of Rin Tin Tin*. He is, perhaps, best remembered nowadays for appearing as Le Chiffre's henchman in the very first adaptation of a James Bond story, the 1954 TV production of *Casino Royale*. He died in August 1958 after undergoing an exploratory operation for lung cancer.

The Episodic Adventures

15. **The Adventure of the Moroccan Hawk-Moth**

Script No. 114
Production No. 2615
Sponsored by Sanka
Release date: 9th January 1957
Written by Siegfried Herzig and Joel Malcolm Rapp
Directed by Phil Rapp
BBC first run 22nd August 1960 at 18:50, repeated 20th July 1961

Cast: Wally Cox (Hiram Holliday), Ainslie Pryor (Joel Smith), Maureen Hingert (Yasmin), Sebastian Cabot (Caid), Mark Dana (Desert Hawk), Than Wyenn (Ahmed)

Synopsis:
Hiram Holliday (Wally Cox) foils an attempt on the lives of four of the free world's leaders.
Hiram is in Morocco hoping to trap a specimen of the Moroccan Hawk Moth but is deterred by a wicked sheik in league with a desert terrorist plotting the assassinations. Hoping to eliminate Hiram, the sheik lures him in to riding a killer stallion—which Hiram quickly tames—then tries to sidetrack him by presenting the bespectacled hero with Yasmin (Maureen Hingert, Miss Ceylon of 1955), the prize of his harem. Hiram resists the temptation and survives a harrowing hour–locked in the harem—and a swordfight with the sheik.

Story:
Hiram and Joel are in Morocco where Hiram is trying to capture the spotted Moroccan Hawk-Moth however instead of capturing a moth he manages to capture a hunting falcon instead. The falcon has a large ornate signet ring in its beak on which Hiram recognises the seal of the 14th Caid of Mekra-bel-Ksiri. Joel leaves in search of food and Ahmed, an emissary appears. He has come to take Hiram to the Caid.

Hiram, and falcon, go to the Caid's Palace and when he is introduced to the rule he calls Hiram "the Hawk"—a desert warrior. Caid wants Hiram to smuggle an explosive into a fort where the four most powerful men in the western world are meeting. Hiram wants to get a message to Joel so the Caid sends Yasmin, from his harem. Joel is busy buying street food when Yasmin approaches him.

Ahmed goes back to see his king. A man has arrived claiming to be the Desert Hawk. When Caid goes to see him he shows him a tattoo of a hawk on his forearm; Caid is convinced. The imposter is an American and whilst Caid suggests they should shower him with gifts, Ahmed suggests that Hiram be killed.

Caid sends Ahmed to get Tabout, his killer stallion, who has already killed three grooms this week. The horse will be his gift to Hiram, who will have to ride it...

Joel arrives just as The Caid and Hiram are in the courtyard waiting for the horse to be brought out. The horse jumps and rears as Hiram gets near it and Joel enters the courtyard nervously, spying the horse. Hiram picks some fruit from a nearby bush but the horse rejects it. But when Hiram starts singing to it, he calms down allowing Hiram to climb on and Joel to breathe a sigh of relief. Caid sends the real Desert Hawk off with the ring and his plans, and decides he will deal with Hiram himself.

Hiram catches up with Joel and tells him about the Caid's plans to blow up the Big Four at their meeting. He sends Joel to go and inform the authorities just as Ahmed comes to collect him and take him to the Caid.

The Caid is sitting at a table full of food as Ahmed ushers Hiram in. Caid invites him to sit down, for he has another gift for him. Two guards enter the room carrying a large rolled up rug, as the rug unrolls Yasmin is revealed. She jumps up and takes a bow. Caid is giving her to Hiram, and they are to be married. She starts a seductive dance.

Joel meanwhile has made contact with Lieutenant Beauchamps of the French Foreign Legion, but Beauchamps does not believe him and tells him that the Caid's palace is out of his jurisdiction anyway.

Back in the palace the meal is over and Yasmin is cuddling up to a distraught Hiram. Yasmin persuades Hiram to go to the garden with her. As they stand and admire the well Ahmed creeps up behind Hiram, intending to tip him over into it, but Hiram realises what's going on, moves out of the way leaving Ahmed to go over the wall and into the well. Yasmin gets Hiram to hide in the Caid's harem and locks him in.

When Yasmin tells the Caid where Hiram is he is furious. He grabs a fierce looking sword off the wall and heads for the harem. But when he gets there the door opens and a number of scantily clad harem girls troop out. Except the last one doesn't look terribly feminine, with a harem outfit over a suit and a veil that doesn't even cover his glasses – it's Hiram!

A fight ensures, the Caid and his sword versus Hiram and his umbrella. The fight moves dangerously close to the well and Hiram stumbles against it, nearly falling in. The Caid spotting an opportunity lunges forward only for Hiram to move out of the way in the nick of time, leaving the Caid diving over the rim of the well.

Joel is still at the fort, tied up with Beauchamps, when Sheil Hasim arrives. Hiram, still dressed as a harem girl and carrying the falcon, barges though security and into the courtyard of the fort. Hasim removes the ring that contains the explosive and hurls it in the direction of the ammo dump nearby. Hiram lets go of the falcon which sails through the sky and catches the ring.

Hasim, determined not to be taken alive, runs off but Hiram, noticing a whip that belonged to his henchman lying on the ground nearby, picks it up and lashes out, catching Hasim around the legs and pulling him to the ground.

The following day Joel is sat in a café, eating, when Hiram walks in. Joel is unhappy as the military have stopped him from publishing his story. Hiram is followed in by the harem girls, whom he is chaperoning to America.

Notes:

Phil Rapp was paid $1,500 for producing and directing this episode, but with all his other responsibilities left the writing of the episode to others.

One of those was his eldest son, Joel Malcolm Rapp. Phil Rapp had eased the way for his son into the industry, commissioning him to write a couple of scripts—under his guidance—for *Topper*, his previous show. Having worked with Hiram "I met a young agent who believed in my ability and told me he could get me a job at Ziv Productions. He was true to his word and I spent the next couple of years working for Ziv...."[35] He wrote scripts for *Highway Patrol*, *Sciene Fiction Theatre* and many other shows. He went on to become a horticultural expert, establishing his own indoor plant business in Hollywood, writing several best-selling books on gardening and cooking and for eleven years appeared alongside Regis Philbin and Kathie Lee Gifford as their resident expert on their day time show.

His co-writer was Siegfried 'Sig' Herzig. A New York native Herzig was born in July 1897 and joined Warner Bros. in the mid-1930s working on more than twenty films for them. He collaborated on the stage production of 'Around the World in Eighty Days' which was presenetd at Jones Beach in conjunction with the 1939 New

---

35 Interview with JMR by Derek Parker Royal

York World's Fair. He moved into television in the 1950s writing for shows such as *The Thin Man*, *Topper* and *Bourbon Street Beat*. He died in March 1985.

Continuing the trend of hiring beauty queens Maureen Hingert had been crowned Miss Ceylon in June 1955. She made her screen debut in October that year in *Pillars of the Sky* for Universal and appeared in handful of TV shows and films. She married her first husband, Mario Armand Zamparelli in 1958 but they divorced in 1970. She married again in 1976 and lived in the San Fernando Valley.

The lovely Yasmin aka Maureen Hingert

16. **THE ADVENTURE OF THE PASTO DURO**

Script No. 117
Production No. 2618
Sponsored by Jello
Release date: 16th January 1957
BBC first run 19th December 1960 at 19:05
Written by Joel Malcolm Rapp
Directed by William J Hole Jr.

Cast:
Wally Cox (Hiram), Ainslie Pryor (Joel Smith), Peggy Hallack (Marita), Joe De Santis (Acosta), Ed Coleman (Zerro), Alberto Mariscal (Raphael)

Synopsis:
Hiram Holliday (Wally Cox) becomes the unwitting tool of international gem thieves.

Enroute to the United States on a vacation from his globe girdling tour, Hiram is duped into carrying stolen diamonds—and, worse, into a phoney marriage, believing he is saving a beautiful girl (Jacqueline Beer) from deportation and a dire fate. Hiram investigates, but is thrown from the ship. Grasping the ships' stern line, he climbs back aboard, and with neat swordsplay more than evens the score with the conspirators.

Notes:
This is another of those episodes for which the script does not exist and no English language version of the programme appears to have survived. However unlike episodes such as 'The Adventure of the Sturmzig Cunieform' there is also no German-dubbed version of this episode currently available.

17. **The Adventure of the Vanishing House**
Script No. 119
Production No. 2619
Sponsored by Jello
Release date: 23rd January 1957
BBC first run 25th December 1960 at 12:05, repeated 26th July 1961
Written by Richard M Powell

Synopsis:
A clever band of French criminals tries to lure Hiram to their side in an attempt to blast into the Bank of France. They propose reaching the blasting spot through a secret tunnel. Hiram reports the plot to the police but each time they approach the house leading to the tunnel, the house vanishes and is replaced by a puppet show. Eventually Hiram manages to get into the tunnel alone to tangle with the gang and save the bank's funds.

BBC Synopsis:

While his friend Joel is busy eating eclairs in Paris, Hiram tries to interest a gendarme in the antics of a Punch and Judy show.

Story:

Hiram and Joel are in Paris and as Joel goes into a pastry shop in search of food, Roxanne, a young pretty French girl runs up to Hiram asking for his help, for her father is in trouble and she can't find the police.

She leads Hiram to a small house where Hiram discovers her father gagged and bound to a chair, with a large ticking bomb beside it. Hiram hold the girl back in the doorway, for he thinks the approach is booby trapped. He lifts up the rug on the floor and shows her a collection of landmines.

Using the top of his umbrella to move them out the way he makes his way to the bomb. Hiram gets his nail clippers out to disarm the explosive but two masked assassins, one with rapier and one with a pistol, advance on Hiram. Using his trusty umbrella he disarms the men and manages to get to the bomb in time to prevent it going off.

Roxanne's father, Cerveau, frees himself from the chair. He's heard of Hiram, and this was a test. Cerveau and his associates are tunnelling into the vault of the Bank of France which adjoins the rear of the building but that is only the start. Cerveau has ambitions, "In six months I shall be the master of France, in a year more the ruler of the Continent or quite dead."

Cerveau wants Hiram by his side but of course Hiram is not interested. He leaves and Roxanne berates Cerveau for letting him go. But Cerveau is playing the long game…

Hiram meets up with Joel outside the pastry shop and tells him what happened. They grab a nearby gendarme and tell him. At first he is sceptical but Hiram takes him and Joel to show them what went on.

But the house has disappeared and been replaced by a Punch & Judy show, being watched by several children. Even Joel is beginning to disbelieve Hiram but Hiram notices that one of the puppets, Punch, looks just like Cerveau. And Judy looks like Roxanne. Clearly something is up but the gendarme is still very sceptical and leaves Hiram and Joel to the puppet show.

Hiram though, can't let it go and decides he has to warn the bank. Cerveau and Roxanne have been performing the puppet show and watch Hiram depart.

At the bank Hiram is talking to Dufeaux when they hear a dull explosion. Dufeaux tells Hiram they are blasting for a new subway tunnel. The explosion gets louder bur Dufeaux is still dismissive. He gets Hiram to show him the puppet show however when they walk back, the show has been replaced by the original house.

Dufeaux is suitably sceptical but follows Hiram as he walks into the house. There Roxanne and Cerveau greet him enthusiastically. Cerveau tells Dufeaux he is a psychiatrist who's been looking after Hiram for some time, Roxanne kisses Hiram—keeping him quiet.

Dufeaux leaves and when Cerveau admits to Hiram that he's kidnapped Joel Hiram goes for the authorities. He manages to find the gendarme from earlier and persuades him to come and see the house, except by the time they get back, the Punch & Judy Show has returned.

They watch the show for a minute and a new puppet emerges in an old-fashioned, formal policeman's outfit, looking just like Joel. Then a puppet looking like Hiram appears...except the gendarme's timing is so bad that he doesn't see it. He's all set to call for medical help for Joel, who is, he thinks, clearly insane.

As the gendarme leaves in search of help Cerveau appears, and Hiram seemingly acquiesces to join him.

Cerveau shows him the tunnel they are digging, which also contains a bound and gagged Joel. Much to Joel's frustration Hiram seems to have completely gone to Cerveau's team. Hiram grabs a stick of dynamite to test it, and soon it becomes clear that Hiram has fooled Cerveau.

With his umbrella in one hand and dynamite in the other Hiram battles Cerveau and his men, manages to free Joel and when he finally tosses the stick of dynamite, break into the vault of the Bank of France...

Notes:
A copy of this episode is held in the Paley Center Collection in the USA however it remains out of circulation and is not currently available.

18. **The Adventure of the Shipwrecked Ancestor**

Script No. 118
Production No. 2616
Sponsored by Sanka
Release date: 30th January 1957
BBC first run 24th August 1960 at 19:05, repeated 28th May 1961
Written by Richard M. Powell
Produced and directed by Philip Rapp

Cast:
Wally Cox (Hiram Holliday, Captain Renaud, Hamid, Malachi, Berber Tribesman, Berber Tribesman's Son, The Professor), Ainslie Pryor (Joel Smith), Stanley Adams (Garreaux), Lita Milan (Marlene)

Synopsis:
Wally Cox plays six different roles in addition to that of Hiram, who seeks records of an ancestor shipwrecked on the African coast in the early 1800s.

During the search Hiram clashes with a ruthless desert sheik over possession of a priceless black box which can convert sea water to fresh water. Joel Smith (Ainslie Pryor), Hiram's pal, is sure the ancestor, Phineas Holliday, got safely ashore, since the natives' faces are unmistakeably stamped with the Holliday features—a fact Hiram stoutly denies. The six new characters played by Cox are Captain Renaud of the French Security Police, Sheik Hamid, an international thief, Malachi, a Viennese scientist, Dr Breuerhof; a Berber tribesman, and the tribesman's nine year old son.

Story:
Hiram and Joel are in North Africa, looking for traces of one of Hiram's ancestors, Phineas Holliday, who was shipwrecked on the coast in 1810 during the war with the Barbary pirates. They have gone to the offices of Captain Renaud, an officer of the French Security Police, for his help.

Renaud, however, doesn't believe them and suggests they're after the story of the black box; "rumors persist of s scientist…a man with a black box. A box that will make the desert bloom like a garden…". Renaud is convinced that Hiram is a criminal but lets them both go.

Hiram and Joel settle into their hotel but unbeknownst to them Garreaux and Marlene are also there.

The criminal duo go to see an elderly Viennese scientist, Dr Breuerhoff who has indeed developed a black box. Garreaux has with him a bucket containing one gallon of sea water. At the Doctor's insistence he pours it in the box. The Doctor grabs a glass and using one of the spigots on the box fills it up...with high octane gasoline. When Garreaux proves it by lighting the fluid the Doctor calmly grabs the glass and puts out the flames with liquid from the second tap – pure fresh water. The third tap outputs a liquid "which contains "every nutritional element"

Garreaux confesses that he is not a representative of the government, as he originally told the Doctor, but his only interest is Garreaux. Whilst the Doctor is clearly altruistic regarding his invention, Garreaux is not. He sends Marlene out of the room and a moment later she hears a shot. Garreaux emerges box in one hand, gun in the other, but as he is talking to Marlene, Malachi comes up behind him and puts a gun in his back. He has been sent by the Sheik and relieves Garreaux of the box before fleeing.

Joel is in a café eating when Hiram joins him, carrying the papers of Abdul Ben Ohmar, the Mediterranean region's greatest authority on shipwrecks, which he hopes will shed light on the mystery of Phineas Holliday.

Malachi enters the café, looking as if he's being pursued. He sits down at Joel's table and tries to sell them the box, but they're not interested. Captain Renaud comes in one door, and Garreaux and Marlene come in another entrance, Malachi tells Hiram and Joel that the box must go to the Sheik, he leaves it on the table, grabs Hiram's papers and leaves. Garreaux, seeing his departure, goes after him.

Captain Renaud sits at Joel's table and tells them of the murder at the hotel, in the room across the hall from theirs.

Garreaux has caught up with Malachi and murdered him. When he returns to Marlene he opens the package Malachi had only to discover it's a collection of papers. They conclude the box must already be in the hands of the Sheik.

Hiram and Joel arrive at the Sheik's palace at the same time as Garreaux and Marlene, whilst they miss each other Joel and Hiram recognise their adversaries. Deciding they need to get rid of the box they place it in the bucket of a nearby well.

Garreaux makes his way to see Sheik Hamid. He offers Marlene as a gift, and starts negotiating with the Sheik, still assuming that the chieftain has the box. Hamid however tells him to go and find the box…or be killed!

Renaud is casually casing the palace and stops at the well for a drink. Joel tries to stop him but Renaud discovers the box and arrests Joel for murder. Garreaux and Marlene watch this from a distance and he sends her to seduce Renaud and get the box.

As the seduction works Garreaux appears, takes the box from Renaud and tosses him into the well.

At a feast that evening Garreaux is tucking in but the Sheik eats nothing, for he simply wants the box and the power it will bring him. Hiram is undercover at the feast as a waiter however Marlene recognises him. But they are interrupted when two bearers knock at the door to collect a carrying litter which is atop a table. At Marlene's behest Hiram climbs on top of the litter, next to the box, and she covers him with a rug. The bearers carry the litter—and Hiram— and place it in front of the Sheik.

Garreaux pulls the rug off it with a flourish and is shocked to discover Hiram. The Sheik takes his scimitar and tries to attack Hiram, who vaults to the other side of the table and grabs a scimitar from one of the bearers. A duel rages around the room, Garreaux grabs his gun but cannot shoot for fear of hitting the wrong man. The duel goes on and Hiram manages to disarm his adversary just as Renaud appears, dripping wet, having climbed out of the well. He arrests everyone.

The following day Hiram and Joel are in the café eating. Hiram is disappointed but Joel is not, after all they got out of jail and they got the papers back. Hiram though has discovered that Phineas Holliday died soon after the shipwreck and left no descendants. Though when a bearded berber and his son come towards their table wearing glasses and carrying umbrellas and looking not a little like Hiram, Joel is not so sure…

Notes:

Phil Rapp was paid $1,500 for producing and directing this episode. Interestingly he was also paid $3,000 for his "services as screen playwright" on this script. Since Richard M Powell is the writer recognised by the Writer's Guild of America for this episode it would seem reasonable to assume that the payment to Rapp was because Powell was blacklisted at the time and originally Rapp took the credit for writing this episode.

Radio and Television Daily[36] liked this episode and the show in general:

"Described as a "technical tour-de-force" by producer-director Phil Rapp, last Wednesday's segment of The Adventures of Hiram Holliday" was just exactly that with a bit of superlative acting by Wally Cox thrown in for good measure. The problems entailed in having Wally portray six different characters might not occur to the casual viewer because of the smoothly flowing manner in which they were done, but it points up the extreme fluidity of the filmed medium. Without stop and go shooting it's certain that this excellent example of TV entertainment would never have been possible.

While no individual scenes caused any extreme heights of hilarity, the entire half hour was loaded with chuckles, a situation which seems to typify the entire series, one which we hope will be around for a long time."

Captain Renaud and Marlene

---

36 4 February, 1957

19.   **The Adventure of the Unkissed Bride**
Script No. 116
Production No. 2617
Sponsored by Jello
Release date: 6th February 1957
BBC first run 25th August 1960 at 19:00, repeated 2nd July 1961
Written by Richard M. Powell

Cast:
Wally Cox (Hiram Holliday), Ainslie Pryor (Joel Smith), Jacqueline Beer (Madeleine), Carl Lindt (Schendel), Robert Boone (Bernhardt), Fredrich Ledebur (Hofdyk)

Synopsis:
Hiram Holliday (Wally Cox) becomes the unwitting tool of international gem thieves. Returning to the US on a vacation from his globe-girdling tour, Hiram is decoyed into carrying stolen diamonds –and is duped into a phony marriage believing he is saving the girl (Jacqueline Beer) from deportation and a dire fate. When he discovers the duplicity he is thrown overboard but climbs back and foils the conspirators.

Story:
In Rotterdam Hiram goes into a toy shop in search of a present for the nephew of a friend. He chooses a concertina and when Schendel the shop keeper offers to add the name in rhinestones on it, we learn the nephew's name, Joel Smith; named after his uncle…

As Hiram is sailing back to New York on the Britannique this evening he arranges to pick it up at three o'clock. As he leaves the shop Schendel calls back to two acquaintances, Bernhardt and Hofdyk, and tells them he has arranged for the diamonds to be shipped to America. They will also sail on the Britannique this evening, along with a French girl, Madeleine, whose job it will be to keep an eye on Hiram by marrying him.

On board the boat Hiram takes a break from unpacking by going for a walk whilst Joel finishes a late evening snack. Schendel is on the deck with Madeleine and proimpted by him she climbs on board one of the railings as if to jump. Hiram rushes to save her and she pretends to be a stowaway, a political refugee. But with no visa she tells Hiram she won't be allowed to land in the USA, hence the plan to jump overboard. She tells Hiram the only way she will get into the country is if she takes his name by getting married. Madeleine and Hiram go off to see the Captain in order to get married.

Bernhardt and Hofdyk drugged the Captain and Hofdyk has borrowed his uniform. Bernhardt tells Schendel that there are two men from Scotland Yard on board, trailing the missing diamonds.

Hiram and Madaleine arrive to see the Captain and, masquerading as the Captain, Hofdyk assures them such a union would not be a problem. Hartley and Shawcross, the two Scotland Yard detectives, get a passenger list from Bernhardt, who's dressed as a steward. Looking at the list Hartley wonder if Schendel could be the smuggler for he has form as a fence but then both Shawcross and Huntley see Hiram's name on the list. And all too familiar with his recent adventures—the theft of the Shahbandar, the Louvre robbery, the Van Hooten affair—they plan to catch him in the act.

Bernhardt, overhearing this, interrupts the wedding ceremony just as Hiram and Madeleine are married. Hofdyk manoeuvres Bernhardt into a sideroom where he tells CShendel that their plan has a problem, Hiram is the world's master thief and they've given the diamonds to him. Schendel decrees they only have one option, to kill Hiram.

Hiram and his new wife head back to the cabin to see Joel. When Hiram breaks the news to him and introduces Madeleine, Joel is so astonished that it's his turn to go for a walk. On deck he runs into Hofdyk, who is still dressed as the Captain. Joel tells him that his friend needs the doctor. When Joel drops Hiram's name, Schendel, Bernhardt and Hofdyk set off to go and see him, leaving Joel trailing behind. They lock Joel in a stateroom and see Hiram singing and playing the concertina to his new wife.

Schendel, convinced Hiram has played him for a fool, sends Bernhardt into get him. They meet on the deck and as Hiram extends his hand to the toymaker Schendel grabs his hand, whirls round, and sends Hiram over the rail.

Madeleine tells Schendel he's made a big mistake, for Hiram had the concertina with him. Meanwhile Hartley and Shawcross are on their way to arrest Hiram when they hear Joel trying to get out of his stateroom. They let him out but once introduction are made they recognise Joel's name and steer him back into the stateroom so that they can have a chat.

As Joel tells them everything that has happened Hiram appears at the doorway, dripping wet. He grabbed a training stern line which helped him get back on the boat.

As Hiram tells what happened Joel explains to him that Schendel and his friends think Hiram's a gem thief. Hiram produces the soggy concertina and explains that what he took for rhinestoens are in fact the missing diamonds. Hofdyk and Bernhardt appear and the two detectives tell Hofdyk, still dressed as the Captain, to arrest him. As they emerge from the stateroom Schendel appears and marches Hiram at gunpoint to the gym.

In the gym Bernhardt starts a fencing duel with Hiram, however whilst Bernhardt has all the safety gear, Hiram does not. But he manages to get the edge on Hofdyk just as the Scotland Yard detectives arrive in the gym, along with the real Captain of the ship.

In New York Joel and Hiram are greeted by Prentice. But Prentice is not happy, for Joel's story makes Hiram sound stupid. Hiram, meanwhile, just wants to visit the Tombs and play chess with Schendel…

Notes:
A copy of this episode is held in the Paley Center Collection in the USA however it remains out of circulation and is not currently available.

Keeping up the stunt casting of beauty queens Parisian born actress and winner of Miss France in 1954 Jacqueline Beer played Mrs Hiram Holliday. She had a slightly longer career in TV than many of her peers who appeared in this show, starring as Suzanne Fabray for five years in the classic private eye show *77 Sunset Strip* But her career petered out in the 1960s and in 1991 she married her second husband, adventurer Thor Heyerdahl. After his death in 2002 she has maintained an interest in the Thor Heyerdahl Research Center in Aylesbury in the UK.

20.   **The Adventure of the Ersatz Joel**
Script No. 122
Production No. 2621
Sponsored by Sanka
Release date: 13th February 1957
BBC first run 26th August 1960 at 19:05, repeated 24th July 1961
Written by Joel Malcolm Rapp

The Episodic Adventures

Cast:
Wally Cox (Hiram Holliday), Ainslie Pryor (Joel Smith), Sebastian Cabot (Cerveau), Carlene King Johnson (Caroline)

Synopsis:
International spies resort to a fiendish ruse through plastic surgery in an attempt to swing Hiram Holliday.

Cerveau (Sebastian Cabot), mastermind of the criminals, uses plastic surgery to make an accomplice identical in appearance to Joel Smith (Ainslie Pryor), Hiram's reporter-friend. The false Joel then attempts to lure Hiram to the side of the spies, but the umbrella-armed hero sees through the dupe when the always-hungry "Joel" refuses extra helpings of food.

BBC Synopsis:
Hiram is forced to join an International Spy Ring operating in New York and is surprised when he discovers that his friend, Joel, is already working for it.

Story:
Hiram and Joel are in New York being watched by Cerveau as they enter the building which houses the offices of the Chronicle. Cerveau is in a different office in the building accompanied by Fritz whose face is swathed in bandages. Cerveau starts to remove them…

In the lift Hiram and Joel are accompanied by Caroline, to whom Joel takes a fancy. But once Joel has left the lift, she forces Hiram at gunpoint to the twenty-sixth floor. Joel doesn't notice and figures Hiram's just gone off to do something. He has, as Caroline takes him to room 2615 where he meets Cerveau, who he thought was still in a Parisian jail.

He wants to go into partnership with Hiram and shows him microfilm of a complete report of the US Defense set-up to try and encourage him. Of course Hiram refuses but then Cerveau shows Fritz into the room. Fritz, sans bandages, looks like Joel and of course Hiram believe he is Joel, and that Joel has gone to the other side. Particularly when the ersatz Joel puts his arm around Caroline and complains about how much Prentice was paying him.

A disillusioned Hiram tells Cerveau he will think his offer over, takes the film and leaves. He goes to see Mr Prentice and tells him he has a story that would be worth holding the front page for, and he has the proof—the film-in his pocket. Just as he's about to explain the problem with the story Joel walks in, but of course the real Joel is clueless as to what Hiram has been up to. And when Hiram goes to show them the film, the film has disappeared.

As Hiram goes back to his desk he sees Cerveau sitting in Joel's office. Hiram asks him how he swapped out the film but Cerveau is not forthcoming. Hiram threatens him with an umbrella to the throat and Cerveau hands over a pen which has the microfilm inside.

Prentice and Joel burst into the office. This isn't Cerveau, he's one of the newspapers biggest advertisers. Hiram vows to take the microfilm to the UN and backs out of the office.

At the UN Hiram goes to see two men, Halifax and Burton. He shows them the pen but there's no film inside. Just a tiny "snake". Burton makes a phone call and confirms that a strip of microfilm containing defense plans has been reported missing.

They accompany Hiram back to the building and go to room 2615 to see Cerveau however it's no longer just an office, it's a hair-dressing salon and Cerveau is the chief stylist. The men from the UN leave and Cerveau tells Hiram he too will be leaving on the Brittanique this evening. The ersatz Joel walks in, and is quickly accompanied by a couple of beautiful girls. A dejected Hiram leaves.

Hiram goes to Joel's office and sees the real Joel, who hasn't a clue what Hiram is talking about. Hiram knocks Joel unconscious to prevent him from leaving.

Hiram goes to see Cerveau on the liner and pretends that he will indeed go into partnership with him. Cerveau hands over the microfilm to him but Hiram is shaken when the ersatz Joel walks in. Following behind him is room service with food and drink but when they all sit down to eat, the ersatz Joel refuses food.

Hiram suddenly gets up and declares he will be going to the authorities with the microfilm. He has seen through the ersatz Joel but Cerveau reveals that the ersatz Joel is an excellent swordsman and pulls a sword from his cane, giving it to Fritz and telling him to kill Hiram.

The sword fight begins, with Hiram parrying Fritz's thrusts using his trusty umbrella. But as the fight moves to the deck Fritz lunges too far, Hiram moves, and the ersatz Joel goes sailing over the rail into the water.

Halifax and Burton take Cerveau away as Hiram hands over the microfilm to them.

Notes:
Beauty queen Carlene King Johnson who plays Caroline in this episode was Miss Vermont of 1953 and Miss USA of 1955. She died in 1969, aged just 35, from illness related to diabetes.

21. The Adventure of Hiram's Holliday
Script No. 121
Production No. 2622
Sponsored by Jello
Release date: 20th February 1957
BBC first run 23rd August 1960 at 19:05, repeated 28th July 1961
Written by Richard M. Powell
Directed by William J Hole Jr.

Cast:
Wally Cox (Hiram Holliday), Ainslie Pryor (Joel Smith), Lee Patrick (Mrs Primrose), John O'Malley (Inspector Shawcross), Ben Wright (Hartley), Lisa Davis (Nurse), Cyril Delevanti (Innkeeper).

Synopsis:
Hiram Holliday, played by Wally Cox, foils a plot to undermine the British economy.
Counterfeiters steal an engraving plate for printing the English pound, their purpose being to flood the country with the fake notes. Scotland Yard detectives accuse Hiram of the felony. To extricate himself from the toils of the law, Hiram must find the real criminals. He finally does, but not before overcoming many hazards.

BBC Synopsis:
While spending a peaceful holiday at a small English hotel, Hiram becomes involved with a gang of forgery experts-and Scotland Yard as well!

Story:

In Ridwick-on-Trent in England, Inspectors Shawcross and Hartley are tracking down a master criminal responsible for stealing a pound-note printing plate that could, in the wrong hands, devastate the British economy. Shawcross suspects that Holliday and Smith are behind the whole thing, but in actuality they are merely there on vacation. However, the other guests at the resort, led by the seemingly innocent Mrs. Primrose, are the criminals responsible for the theft of the plate. Mrs. Primrose tricks Holliday into giving her a plan for smuggling the plate into the resort unnoticed.

Mrs. Primrose lures Shawcross and Hartley to the post office, where Holliday is picking up a package that they believe contains the stolen plate. Disguised as robbers, they try to take the package from him by force but he knocks them unconscious. During the commotion, Mrs. Primrose slips in and grabs her own package before leaving. Shawcross and Hartley reveal themselves and arrest Holliday. Upon being questioned by the police, Holliday reveals that his package merely contained an assortment of seashells. Mortified, they begrudgingly release Holliday from custody.

Holliday starts to become suspicious of the other guests, realizing he must solve the case in order to clear his name. He passes on his suspicions that Mrs. Primrose is the one with the stolen plate to Shawcross and Hartley, but she appears with a package of treacle, thus establishing an alibi. Still suspicious, Holliday searches her room but finds one of the guests' nurses there. She gives him the package, double-crossing Mrs. Primrose. She tries to convince him to run away with her and keep the plate for themselves, becoming rich. They are interrupted by Mrs. Primrose arriving with Smith at gunpoint.

After sending Shawcross and Hartley away, Mrs. Primrose plans to take Holliday, Smith, and the nurse out back to murder them, and is accompanied by the other guests, all armed. Using a timely distraction, Holliday and Smith are able to escape their captors and incapacitate all of them. The episode ends as Shawcross and Hartley arrive just in time for Holliday to hand them the package and leave them to arrest the criminals.

Notes:
A copy of this episode is held in the Paley Center Collection in the USA however it remains out of circulation and is not currently available.

Versatile character actress Lee Patrick was born in New York in 1901. Inspired by her father who was the editor of a trade paper she developed an interest in theatre at a young age. She made her Broadway debut in November 1922 as part of the ensemble cast in the Jerome Kern and Anne Caldwell musical *The Bunch and Judy* and appeared in shows such as *The Green Beetle, June Moon, Little Women, Blessed Event* and *Stage Door* before signing a contract with RKO which led to her film debut in the 1929 film *Strange Cargo*. She went on to make more than two hundred films and starred on Broadway with many names before they hit the big time including Spencer Tracy, Humphrey Bogart, Fatty Arbuckle and Jimmy Stewart. Perhaps her most famous role was as Effie, the Girl Friday to Humphrey Bogart's Sam Spade in the classic 1941 film *The Maltese Falcon* but the one that got her the job on this show was almost certainly that of Mrs Topper on *Topper*. She died in 1982 of a heart seizure, the day before her seventy-first birthday.

The marvellous Ben Wright who played Hartley was born in London in May 1915 and studied acting at the Royal Academy of Dramatic Arts. He began acting professionally in 1934 with a number of stage roles in London's West End but like so many his career was interrupted when war broke out. He enlisted and served in the Kings Royal Rifle Corps. In 1946 he went to America to attend a cousin's wedding and settled in Hollywood. His talent for dialects meant he quickly found work in radio and he went on to appear on shows such as *The New Adventures of Sherlock Holmes, Suspense, The Voyage of the Scarlet Queen, Escape* and *The Adventures of Philip Marlowe*. His film and TV career started in earnest in the late 1940s with a number of uncredited roles but he was soon guesting in shows such as *Playhouse 90, The Third Man, Have Gun – Will Travel* and *Perry Mason*. He also did voice-over work, notably in Disney's *101 Dalmatians, The Jungle Book* and the 1989 film *The Little Mermaid*. He died in July 1989 due to complications from heart bypass surgery.

22.   The Adventure of the Misguided Missile
Script No. 120
Production No. 2620
Sponsored by Jello
Release date: 27th February 1957
BBC first run 20th December 1960 at 19:05, repeated 25th July 1961
Written by Richard M. Powell

Cast:
Wally Cox (Hiram Holliday), Ainslie Pryor (Joel Smith), Stanley Adams (Garreaux), Lita Milan (Marlene), Marcel Rousseau (Professor De Musset)

Synopsis:
Trying to keep the first earth satellite from falling into the hands of the criminal Garreaux (Stanley Adams), Hiram Holliday, played by Wally Cox, runs afoul of the French Surete.

Garreaux kills an eminent French scientist to become owner of the satellite. A quick switch in baggage checks delivers the satellite to Hiram and an Aepyornis egg to Garreaux. The master criminal and his accomplice, Marlene (Lita Milan) pursue Hiram, retrieve the satellite briefly, then lose all in a derring-do duel on the stage of the Paris Opera House. Joel Smith (Ainslie Pryor), Hiram's reporter-friend, shows up late as usual.

Story:
Hiram is in Madagascar, at the airport, checking in for a flight to Paris complete with an egg. He goes to send a telegram but at the telegraph desk De Musset, a nervous, elderly man, starts talking to him and tells him that they must swap identity papers for De Musset is being followed and what is in his bag must get to Paris, for the peace of the world. They swap papers.

Also at the airport are Garreaux and Marlene, who are the ones following De Musset. Joel is in Paris, in the office of Inspector Ducasse. Ducasse tells Joel that De Musset is bringing to Paris the first complete earth satellite but no one knows what de Musset looks like, for he will accept no police protection. Ducasse also thinks that Hiram's gone to Madagascar to steal the satellite whilst Joel maintains that Hiram went to look for the egg of the Aepyornis bird.

The police intercept a telegram for Joel at his hotel. It's from Hiram telling Joel he will arrive in Paris this evening "with the greatest prize of my career" which of course Ducasse misinterprets.

On the airplane Garreaux spies a familiar looking umbrella and realises that Hiram is aboard. He goes to meet the owner of the umbrella only to discover that, of course, it is not Hiram. Marlene apologises for him, and thinks Garreaux is obsessed.

Joel and Ducasse are at Orly but discover the flight has been diverted to Bourges due to fog. All the passengers are decamping at Bourges and staying in a hotel overnight, travelling on to Paris in the morning. At the airport Garreaux passes Hiram but shaken by his earlier encounter with the umbrella, thinks he is seeing things. And when the attendant calls him Monsieur Holliday Marlene thinks he is hearing things.

At the hotel Marlene and Garreaux are in a room opposite Hiram's. They have what they believe is de Musset's bag but when they open it they discover an egg, Hiram's egg.

Hiram is in his hotel room examining the satellite when Joel bursts in. he tells Hiram that the police are after him because they think he went to Madagascar to steal a satellite…then he notices what Hiram is examining. Hiram tells Joel what happened and decides they need to deliver it to the French High Command in Paris.

Garreaux and Marlene catch up with Hiram and Joel as they leave their respective hotel rooms. Garreaux shuffles them back into Hiram's room at gunpoint.

Ducasse knocks on Hiram's door and Garreaux gets Hiram to let him in. Despite Joel's protestations that it is Garreaux holding them at gunpoint Ducasse doesn't believe him, for they have received word from Madagascar that Garreaux's body has been found and Ducasse is assuming he was killed by Hiram.

Garreaux hands over 'his' passport to Ducasse; he is of course Professor de Musset, and Marlene is his niece. Ducasse arrests Joel and Hiram. However with the aid his trusty umbrella Joel and Hiram make their escape.

At the Paris Opera House Hiram is dressed in the armour of Lohengrin, though it's fair to say Lohengrin never carried an umbrella before. Marlene entices him into a dressing room and shows him both the satellite and the Aepyornis egg which are in a trunk in the room.

As Marlene leaves the dressing room, Garreaux, dressed as a spear carrier for the opera, enters. Hiram manages to persuade Garreaux that he is in fact Hiram and gets him to leave the dressing room carrying the egg. Marlene breaks the illusion and both she and Garreaux go after Hiram.

However our hero as made his escape on to the stage where the opera is in full flow. With Hiram using his umbrella to defend himself a fight ensues that is ended when Ducasse arrives and the curtain comes down. Ducasse apologises, for they have verified Hiram's story.

23.   **The Adventure of the Surplus General**
First run on TV in USA (syndication): December 11th, 1959
BBC first run 19th June 1961 at 19:05
Written by Richard M. Powell
Directed by Phil Rapp

BBC Synopsis:
The intrepid Hiram finds himself in trouble when he impersonates a general in order to help a princess.

The King of Borokavia is imprisoned by his arch-enemy and Hiram disguises himself to rescue him.

Story:
Holliday and Smith arrive in the Balkan nation of Barokovia to do an article on beekeeping. However, Holliday is called to the palace by Princess Heidi on apparently urgent matters. He and Smith answer her call, only to find that she is engaged to Baron Schwanfeld, the man who had previously kidnapped King Peter. She seems quite content with the arrangement, but when Holliday leaves he finds that Heidi has slipped him a note informing him that Schwanfeld has imprisoned King Peter and is bringing in a foreign general named Von Plotzen to lead the army of Barokovia upon Schwanfeld's ascension to the throne. Holliday sends Smith to contact the paper while he goes to see Von Plotzen, whom they had unknowingly met earlier that morning.

Holliday visits Von Plotzen, who quickly discerns his identity and holds him at gunpoint. Holliday knocks him unconscious and steals his various medals and decorations in order to disguise himself as Von Plotzen. Thus disguised, he meets with Schwanfeld and demands to see Peter in the dungeon. Once there, he secretly communicates his true identity to Peter as part of a plan to rescue him from the dungeon. In accordance with Holliday's plan, Peter pretends to lash out at Holliday. Heidi meets Schwanfeld and the disguised Holliday outside of the dungeon, expressing her obvious contempt for them both and her love for Holliday, much to Holliday's surprise.

At Schwanfeld and Heidi's engagement party, Holliday secretly reveals his true identity to her, hatching a plan to escape the country with her and Peter. Meanwhile, the real Von Plotzen arrives and proves his identity to Schwanfeld by showing him his family ring. Schwanfeld and Von Plotzen expose Holliday and throw him in the dungeon with Peter; he is scheduled to be executed in the morning. Heidi manages to visit Holliday; she stole Von Plotzen's ring and used it to convince the guards that she was sent by him. With her assistance, Holliday breaks the three of them out of the cell and they adopt disguises in order to sneak out of the castle.

Von Plotzen and Schwanfeld realize his ring has been stolen. Smith is arrested for attempting to send out a dispatch. Soon Holliday is exposed and he and Smith fight off the guards in a swordfight. They get Von Plotzen and Schwanfeld to surrender and the day is saved. The episode ends as Peter bestows Holliday with the title of "Sir Hiram of the Umbrella."

Notes:
A copy of this episode is held in the Paley Center Collection in the USA however it remains out of circulation and is not currently available.

24. **The Adventure of the Diamond Eater**
Produced and directed by Philip Rapp
Written by Richard Powell
First aired in US syndication on 18 December, 1959
First run on BBC 21st December 1960 at 18:50, repeated 27th July 1961

Cast: Wally Cox (Hiram Holliday), Ainslie Pryor (Joel Smith), Lita Milan, Stanley Adams, John O'Malley, Ben Wright

BBC Synopsis:
Returning by train to his village for the ancient ceremony of being weighed in diamonds, an Indian Rajah is disposed of and replaced by an international diamond thief. Unfortunately for the imposter Hiram is on the same train.

Hiram foils a plot by an imposter pretending to be a Hindu potentate, who claims he is owed tribute of his weight in diamonds.

25. **The Adventure of the Amontillado**
Unaired on NBC,
Aired on 20th March 1959 on CBC

Show on the BBC on 20th June 1961, at 19:05
Written by Phil Rapp

BBC Synopsis:
Hiram is accused of attempting to assassinate the Prime Minister of France. With the aid of hypnotism, ju-jutsu, and his umbrella, Hiram sets out to find the real culprits.

Story:
Hiram and Joel are on the French Riviera watching the welcoming parade for the Prime Minister when a young girl pushes between them with a gun and fires a few shots at the PM. Hiram grabs the gun off her and she disappears back into the crowd. They try to give chase but are arrested by Inspector Ducasse who believes they are the assassins.

On a yacht offshore the girl, Gina, joins Garreaux and an artistic-looking European man, Prochek. Gina sets up Hiram and Joel so that Garreaux and his cronies can get into their room, which happens to be right next door to that of the Prime Minister. Garreaux is planning to kidnap the politician.

Ducasse goes to perform a ballistics test in front of Hiram and Joel to demonstrate their guilt but when the test fails, Hiram points out that the gun was full of blanks. Hiram and Joel leave custody.

Under the guise of being an artist Garreaux and his gang move into Hiram's hotel room. The concierge acquiesces as he believes Hiram and Joel are still in jail. Garreaux spots Hiram's umbrella in a corner of the room and breaks it in half.

Hiram and Joel arrive back at the hotel to discover they've been evicted. The concierge declares them an enemy of France so Hiram goes to his room to retrieve his umbrella. He discovers Prochek and Gina pretending to be artist and model and leaves. Hiram vaguely recognises Gina but can't place her.

Ducasse spies Joel watching the furore around the PM and making notes for his story. He leads him away from the crowd.

Garreaux and Procheck meanwhile have made a hole in the wall of their hotel room and are almost through to the Prime Minister's room. Joel catches up with Hiram as he realises where he'd seen Gina before. They grab Ducasse and head back to the hotel.

Gina tells the policeman she recognises Hiram from when he shot the gun and with Procheck and Gina masquerading as members of the UN Security Police, Joel and Hiram are not out of trouble yet. Prochek says they need to keep hold of Hiram to question him. Despite Joel's protestations Ducasse agrees and he and Joel leave.

Garreaux reveals himself, and a drugged Prime Minister, to Hiram. He tells Prochek and Gina to take him to the yacht. When they are alone Garreaux shows Hiram a pile of bricks and mortar. Garreaux draws parallels with the Edgar Allen Poe tale The Cask of Amontillado, which Hiram is familiar with. In that story which featured two friends, one was walled up in a catacomb by the other.

At the police station with Joel, Ducasse phones the UN Police and to Joel's amusement Ducasse is told there is no such Captain Prochek and realises the truth. Garreaux, meanwhile, is busy bricking Hiram into a recess in the wall but Hiram manages to hypnotise him and get him to knock the bricks down and escapes.

Hiram makes his way on to the yacht but is about to be overpowered by Prochek and two crewmen when Garreaux arrives, he has come to watch the demise of Hiram Holliday. Hiram fights his way through the goons and manages to throw Garreaux overboard however the PM, who has emerged from his cabin to see what's going on, suffers the same treatment from an enthusiastic Hiram.

Notes:
Filmed from 12 Feb-14 Feb 1957 this episode had a total budget of $37,926. Curiously one of the gendarmes in the police station is called Maigret. Perhaps Phil Rapp was a fan of Georges Simenon.

26.   **The Adventure of the Invisible Man**
Unaired on NBC
Written by Richard Powell
Directed by Phil Rapp
BBC first run 21st June 1961 at 19:05

BBC Synopsis:
Hiram adds a new trick to his amazing repertoire of the impossible; the ability to make himself invisible. It proves particularly useful to his friend Joel who has just taken up boxing.

Story:

Hiram is in New York back at work at the newspaper. Joel walks into the office looking disappointed, for he's been demoted because of the poor quality of the stories he filed whilst travelling around the world with Hiram. And much to his disgust he's been demoted to sports...

He sits down at his desk, next to Hiram and starts rifling through some of his stories determined to provide his editor wrong but he falls asleep...

When he wakes up he can hear Hiram but he can't see him. Hiram tells him it's a little invention he's been working on...the power to make himself invisible. Joel declares it the greatest invention in the world and starts to imagine all its uses but Hiram's not convinced.

Prentice walks up to Joel, who promptly tells him about Hiram's invention. But when Hiram doesn't respond Prentice tells Joel to stop clowning around and go and interview the European heavyweight boxer, The Great Grodowski, who's staying at the Plaza Hotel. Invisible Hiram returns, having been to the water cooler, and offers to go with Joel. Hiram grabs his umbrella as they leave.

At the Plaza Grodowski's door is answered by Garreaux whom Joel vaguely recognises but can't place. Garreaux introduces himself saying "When you interview me, you interview Grodowski" and shows them Grodowski training with a punchbag in another room. Garreaux, annoyed by a question from Hiram, tells him to disappear.

So he does. And then goes to punch the bag which freaks Garreaux out. And when Invisible Hiram picks up the umbrella Garreaux starts chasing it only to bump into Marlene as she enters the room. Invisible Hiram puts the umbrella down leaving Marlene to wonder if Garreaux has been on the wine again.

Garreaux introduces Joel to Marlene Nicole, star of stage and screen and Joel vaguely recognises her, but again can't quite figure out where from. Marlene is to marry Grodowski but when Joel queries the beautiful Marlene marrying him, well an ape, Grodowski takes offence and goes to punch Joel, only for Invisible Hiram to punch him.

Garreaux kicks Joel out of the hotel room. But as he leaves Marlene catches up with him and tells him that she's not marrying for love, she's marrying because she has family in Grodowski's country and they won't be safe unless she marries the ape.

Joel and Hiram plot to use Hiram's invention to help make Joel the boxing champion

We cut to the boxing ring. At the end of round one 'Phantom' Smith, the new heavy-weight sensation is having an argument with his manager but is getting ready for round two. As the bell goes Hiram and Joel rush into the ring. Invisible Hiram punches Tiger Tom with a number of unseen jabs. Soon it's "another sensational knockout for Phantom Smith, the Fighting Reporter!"

In Cincinnatti Joel wins fight number eight, in Milwaukee, number nine and soon he's on his way to New York to fight Grodowski.

Marlene visits Joel, who's busy training for the big fight, only to be interrupted by Garreaux. Garreaux offers Joel a million dollars to lose the fight, yet still save Marlene. Joel refuses, and Garreaux believes him to be a fake.

Just before the fight Joel tells Hiram that once he's beaten Grodowski he's going to be engaged to Marlene. Garreaux brings the boxing commissioner into the changing room, convinced he knows the truth about how Joel has been so successful—he has an invisible assistant. The commissioner looks at Garreaux...he's clearly losing it.

When the fight starts Grodowski lands a lucky punch which knocks out Hiram. Then Grodowski lands another punch and Joel joins Hiram on the canvas. But they come to their senses, Hiram disappears again and soon Joel is the new heavyweight king of the world.

Prentice climbs into the ring shouting for Joel's attention as we cut back to the newspaper office and Prentice trying to wake Smith up...

Notes:
Powell received $2,500 for writing this episode whilst Phil Rapp received $500 as per their agreement. Rapp also received $1,500 for directing this episode and a royalty payment of $250 per show.

A number of stories were scripted and indeed registered with the Writers Guild of America, but never produced due to the premature cancellation. These include The Adventure of Pandora's Box, The Adventure of the Rustled Rocket and The Adventure of the Treasure Trove.

The Adventure of Pandora's Box
Written by Richard M Powell

Story:

Hiram is in London, admiring the works of art at the British Museum. It is near closing time and with the guards starting to lock up, Hiram is making the most of his last few minutes and is admiring a remarkably lifelike statue when it falls off its pedestal. He catches it in his arms but is even more surprised when it turns to him and says "Kiss me". He does, and is even more confused when the statue says she, Pandora, has been waiting three thousand years for him. He leaves quickly. Round the corner he bumps into a security guard. When Hiram tells him what happened the guard seems remarkably accepting, although maintains a sense of humor about it, suggesting Hiram needs some fresh air. Hiram asks him to take a look at the statue but there is nothing but the pedestal the status was stood on.

Hiram is arrested for stealing the statue and taken to Scotland Yard where he is interviewed by Hartley and Shawcross. Hiram, being Hiram, walks out of the interview, saying he'll look for evidence so they can convict him.

Albert, a workman from the museum delivers a crate to Schmidlapp in his hotel room. Albert tells him everything went to plan; he wheeled the girl in and wheeled the statue out. Schmidlapp opens the crate but Pandora arrives and tells him what happened with Hiram. Schmidlapp is not upset, it means rather than returning the statue they simply need to dispose of it.

Schmidlapp reveals that there's a box in the statue, a "device of priceless value" but when he examines the statue the box is gone. They think it must have been Hiram who stole it and Pandora leaves to seduce it back from him.

Hiram goes back to his hotel room only to find Pandora waiting for him. They talk, with Pandora still pretending to be the statue come to life and Hiram trying to rationalise it, when Joel enters. Hiram tells him what happened but when he asks Pandora to confirm everything she tells Joel that Hiram is mad. She curls up on the sofa and goes to sleep.

At a hotel across the street Schmidlapp watches Hiram and Joel's room whilst down in the street Shawcross and Hartley are also watching the room. Joel spies the two detectives but with Pandora asleep and nothing else seemingly to be done, he goes to lie down. As he leaves the room Pandora wakes up. As she talks to Hiram she reaches behind the sofa and pulls out a small black box and from it produces a diamond, about fifty carats, which she gives to Hiram.

The box makes diamonds according to Pandora but when she tells Hiram they must flee together with the box an argument ensues; Joel wakes up and Hiram tells him what happened. He goes to get Hartley and Shawcross. Hiram persuades them to come up to his room, but Albert and Schmidlapp have beaten them to it and are not happy when they learnt has Hiram has gone for the police. Schmidlapp concludes Hiram must have hidden the box at the museum and at gunpoint, hurries Joel down the fire escape to go with them. This, of course, is just before Hiram and the police get to the room, and discover no one's in it. When Hiram spies the letter M that Joel has written in the dust, he concludes they've gone to the museum. Shawcross and Hartley try to arrest Hiram but he makes his escape with the aid of his trusty umbrella.

At the museum Hiram founds a bound and gagged Joel, and an armed Schmidlapp and Albert find Hiram. A furious fight is interrupted by Shawcross and Hartley who burst in, guns drawn. Hiram takes the gag from Joel and they tell the policemen everything, leaving them to arrest the trio.

The Adventure of the Rustled Rocket.

Story:

Hiram and Joel are in trouble. They've been captured by Pancho Salazar and his men and are being held, hands tied on horseback, underneath a tree. Just as the nooses are placed around their necks, Lauran Chambers, a young rancher arrives.

Salazar is punishing Hiram and Joel as they were caught rustling animals from her herd. But when Lauran threatens to to go the sheriff about Salazar's treatment of the men she too is captured by Salazar. Whilst Salazar is busy doing that Hiram recalls how they got in this mess...

One day, when both Hiram and Joel were in the newspaper offices, Joel gets a letter about an uncle who's left him a ranch in the West. Joel assumes they're going to be rich with "Huge herds of cattle, oil, gold,...uranium maybe..." When Prentice storms out of his office calling Joel's latest work "the worst piece of drivel I have ever seen" Joel, believing himself to be a millionaire ranch owner, quits at the same time Prentice fires both of them.

The Lazy S Ranch, Joel's inheritance, is in New Mexico. Salazar is having dinner with Dr Nutrov in the ranch house. He has stolen an atomic rocket from the US Government and is keeping it on the ranch. Dr Nutrov has been hired to set off the rocket. Salazar is negotiating with the government and if negotiations fail, well he plans to launch the rocket at Washington and destroy the government.

Joel and Hiram arrive and after introductions are made, Salazar invited them to sit down to dinner. Laura arrives with an instant dislike for Joel as she claims his uncle stole all her father's cattle. Joel denies Uncle Henry but Laura won't listen and storms out.

After dinner Joel and Hiram are unpacking. Joel pulls out a Geiger counter and discovers a fairly steady reading, suggesting there is uranium in the neighbourhood. They explore the site using the Geiger counter and Joel is convinced he's going to be rich, with all the uranium he believes is on the ranch. Back at the ranch help Joel cannot help but share the news with Salazar who offers to go with him to the uranium, along with Doctor Nutrov.

As they explore the ranch Salazar sneaks off, opens a gate to Laura's ranch and tosses a rock at her cattle, believing they will trample Joel and Hiram. As the stampede charges towards them Hiram tells Joel to get off his horse and lie flat on the ground, since stamping cattle will avoid a prostrate human at all costs.

It works, but as they pick themselves up from the dirt Laura arrives and believes Joel and Hiram were trying to steal her cattle.

Back under the tree with attention centred on Laura, Hiram has managed to untie his hands and manages to free Joel and removes the nooses just as Salazar scares their horses. Hiram and Joel, who's never ridden a horse speed off and Laura's not far behind. Salazar and his cronies give chase. Hiram is an excellent horseman and manages to prevent an out of control Joel from riding straight over a cliff.

Just as they all take a breath Salazar starts shooting at them. The chase continues, with Hiram taking the leading horse. They take cover in a clump of trees but discover more than they bargained for, for that is where Salazar has hidden the rocket. Hiram, realising it is an atomic rocket, disarms it.

Salazar launches the rocket but it explodes in mid-air. As he and his cronies watch the explosion Hiram, Joel and Laura hold them at gunpoint but Salazar causes Hiram to demonstrate what a good shot he is.

As Hiram and Joel are packing to go back to New York, we discover that Prentice has reconsidered and taken them back. And the US Government has paid them a sizeable reward.

Also written and not produced was **THE ADVENTURE OF THE PALEOZOIC EGG** by Donn Mullally

The Episodic Adventures

Prentice is at home by the pool, dictating a typically angry memo to Joel, who's in Chilecito, Argentina. Smith listens to the end of the message in his tent, cold, unshaven, very sorry for himself. Prentice's sign-off of "Go forth to adventure and romance my boy!" does not inspire him.

He's in the peaks of the Andes. Joel, as you might expect, is dressed appropriately for the weather, Hiram is not. With his umbrella by his side and a scarf round his neck he's busy digging in the rocks. But his diggings has consequences and starts an avalanche. Joel and Hiram take shelter in the hole that Hiram has been digging and survive the chaos. As they climb out they spy an egg which has been left uncovered by the avalanche. Whilst Joel envisages a king-sized omelette Hiram realises it's a paleozoic egg. This is an important discovery and he tells Joel they must go and quickly file a story on it.

They head to the telegraph office in Chilecito, however Juan tells them the lines are down so they can't send anything. Marita spies on them from the back room and watches as Hiram and Joel leave. Which is good, for she is guarding a man who is gagged and tied to a chair. Juan comes in and continues to torture the man.

At a landing strip hacked out of the jungle a WWII surplus plane arrives. In the airstrip office three people have been tied up by General Ricardo Vasquez a dictator in waiting. A clean-cut young man in a leather jacket exits the plane and makes his way to the office only for one of Vasquez's goons to knock him unconscious as he enters the building. Vasquez wants to leave once Marita and Juan are finished.

Hiram and Joel arrive at the aircraft hanger and ask Cholito, one of Vasquez's men, if they can charter a flight to Buenos Aires. Cholito, who looks ill, tells them the plane is already booked. Hiram and Joel head to the office where the General and his men are making a show of staffing the place. Hiram tells him their flight will be delayed as their pilot looks ill. Cholito, who's followed them into the office, collapses and Vasquez is at a loss as to what to do until Hiram volunteers his services as a pilot. Hiram however discovers there's no room for Joel—or the egg—on the plane.

Once they are underway Vasquez forces Hiram at gunpoint to change course and land at Maltoroo instead of Buenos Aires. Hiram protests but Vasquez insists, until they hit turbulence which parts Vasquez from his gun. Hiram grabs it and Vasquez returns to the cabin, panting and trembling.

Marita goes into the cabin, intent on seducing Hiram. She plants a magnet she's taken from her vanity case under the instrument panel which of course has an effect on the compass. When she stops smothering Hiram with her affection he looks at the compass and thinks they've gone way off course so compensates. When he lands the plane he discovers they're at Maltorro Airport and not in Buenos Aires.

He breaks the news to the other passengers but Juan produces his gun and raps Hiram on the back of the head leaving him unconscious. The General and his staff disembark the plane leaving Hiram and a bomb, behind. He comes to and discovers the bomb with just ten seconds left. He places it gently on the plane and runs like hell towards the airport. The plane explodes in the background.

Hiram runs almost straight into a policeman who arrests him, believing him to be an anarchist.

Vasquez reads of Hiram's arrest in the newspaper and is annoyed for no one—at this stage—must know he's still alive. He wants to take over the country and later, the whole of South America! But for that to happen Hiram Holliday cannot be in the hands of the police.

Hiram is being interrogated by Regas, a Spanish speaking policeman. He doesn't believe Hiram's tale but further interrogation is interrupted as the Minister of Justice, Doctor Zarraca, wants a word with Hiram.

Juan, and another of Vasquez's goons, arrive to take Hiram. Regas assumes they're going to take him to the Minister despite Hiram's protestations so lets them go. A moment after they have left Doctor Zarraca himself arrives. Regas realises his mistake and starts weeping...

There is a fiesta in the streets and Hiram and his captors are forced to get out of the car and walk. But as they do Hiram gets separated from them by a massive conga line. He takes advantage of his good fortune and makes his escape.

Vasquez goes out into the streets to look for Hiram and sees Inspector Regas and his Minister doing the same. Hiram is busy doing the conga in a nearby ballroom when Vasquez finds him. They fight but Regas and Zarraca enter the ballroom. Hiram manages to escape and runs to a nearby cable car terminal where one is about to depart. He gets into the cable car, which pulls away just as Regas and the police arrive. But when Hiram turns to sit down, he finds Vasquez is already in the car. Vasquez is annoyed, Hiram has cost him his revolution. He pulls out his dagger and starts attacking Hiram. Hiram parries his blows with his umbrella.

The Episodic Adventures

A charge from Vasquez carries them both outside the cable car and soon the fight moves to the roof of the cable car. Just as it seems Vasquez is about to dispose of Hiram over the side Holliday leaps to the roof of a cable car passing in the opposite direction. Vasquez follows him over but loses his balance. He pulls out his bola to try and eliminate Hiram but Hiram uses his umbrella to capture him instead and presents a captured Vasquez to the police at the cable terminal.

Joel eventually catches up with Hiram at the hotel only to discover it wasn't a paleozoic egg, but an ostrich one, and it's hatched...

Prior to cancellation Phil Rapp documented his plans for future adventures for Hiram:

"Aside from the wealth of incident and character studies in Paul Gallico's book, the following ideas can easily be applied and bent into comic and adventurous form.

Hiram in the circus: In hiding from both the Marlene gang and the police, Hiram hides his identity behind the disguise of Grognolle the clown. The action reaches a peak when his disguise is unmasked and a chase on the high wire and trapeze results.

Hiram at Monte Carlo. A mathematical system for winning at roulette gets him in trouble with the management of the casino, who seek to have him eliminated. Other interests even more unscrupulous seek to get the secret for their own uses, and Hiram finds himself between two fires. His knowledge of savate, plus a remarkable display of surgical skill, necessary when his confidante, Smith, is injured by gunshot serves to stamp Hiram again as the most gifted man in the world.

Hiram in Graustark. A plot to kidnap the young heir to the throne involves Hiram, the events being further complicated by the fact that Hiram bears almost a twin resemblance to the prime mover of the plot, the Black Prince of Graustark. A dual role, of course.

Hiram and the air pirates. A European airliner bearing some vastly important strategic war materials as well as cargo of passengers is taken over in midair by the Marlene gang. After the passengers are parachuted out by force, the gang seeks to divert the course of the plane to the country in whose service they are currently engaged. The pilot and navigator make their escape by chute, and the gang is forced to beg Hiram to take over the controls when the plane goes into a deadly spin.

Hiram and the idol's eye. The temple idol of an obscure Asiatic country turns up with a five hundred carat eye missing, and Hiram finds himself in danger of being put in the same condition unless he can clear himself by tracking down the stolen gem. In doing so he is forced to call into play his amazing knowledge of temple dancing, tiger tracking, the almost unknown mystic religious rites of the East, and the complete art of the lapidary.

Hiram and the diplomat's wife. An international incident threatens serious repercussions when the wife of a European envoy announces she is leaving her husband for the fascinating American, Hiram Holliday. Hiram is challenged to a duel with misericords, or the traditional dagger of mercy, and is forced to fight off an ambuscade when the true purpose of the duel and the romance is revealed.

Hiram and the tramp steamer. As a passenger on a harmless tramp steamer, Hiram uncovers the fact that the ship is carrying explosives sufficient to blow up the largest seaport in any part of the globe, and in fact this is the intention of the captain and the crew. Left alone and in chains on the steamer, with the crew over the side in lifeboats and the course set for a major port, Hiram is fully extended before bringing about a peaceful solution.

Hiram in Spain. A beautiful but unscrupulous senorita almost puts an end to the adventures of Hiram Holliday, but the most gifted man in the world thwarts the doll and her co-conspirators, using a fantastic exhibition of bull-fighting and flamenco dancing to save his skin.

Obviously, the world is Hiram's oyster. There is no place on earth, or in space either, for that matter – no situation, no art or skill, that cannot be employed in the manufacture of a rollicking adventure for Hiram and his vis-à-vis, reporter Joel Smith.

Chapter Five: The Afterlife of Hiram Holliday

> *"I thought Hiram was one of the best series of all time in that it was a highly intelligent James Bond. Wally Cox was a unique character. I think that today it would still make a great series or motion picture. I always felt that the time slot was its downfall. Plus, it cost so much money to make it as a TV show then, since the sets and locations had to change every week."*
>
> Paul Rapp as quoted in *The Gripes of Rapp*
> (Ben Ohmart, Bearmanor Media)

Young & Rubicam executive Rod Erickson still had faith in both Hiram Holliday and Phil Rapp and, post-cancellation, set up a meeting between Rapp and Hannah Weinstein of Sapphire Films in London in June 1957. Weinstein was an American producer who had decamped to Great Britain and had a number of series running on the newly formed ITV network (*The Adventures of Robin Hood*, *The Adventures of Sir Lancelot* and *The Buccaneers* were the early ones).

Erickson called Hiram "probably ahead of its time in television, but would make an excellent vehicle for Alec Guinness in a fast-moving feature movie." Rapp also took the opportunity to pitch his pilot for *Merlin the Magician (King Arthur's Court)* which he'd shot back in February and starred Bert Lahr as well as his ongoing struggle to get *The Bickersons* on television.

Erickson reportedly emphasized Rapp's British heritage and the fact that he could get access to finance in the UK as well but sadly nothing came of the discussions.

A shame, because Rapp would have fit in well with Weinstein's shows almost all of which had solid transatlantic appeal.

But as you might expect from a character whose adventures have appeared in magazine and book form as well as on TV, Hiram's story does not end there. However at a time when established characters are being rebooted and reimagined and adapted into all sorts of new media, Hiram's story doesn't go quite where you might expect.

The TV series not long after the initial network broadcast and one of the first buyers was sold to the CBC network in Canada who brought the show in September 1958. Another early purchaser was WPIX in New York, then an independent station that had only been on air since June 1948; they brought the full package of twenty-six episodes, including those that were never broadcast by NBC and started running it weekly on Thursday nights in March 1959.

They weren't the only ones. *The Adventures of Hiram Holliday* started to travel all around the globe; the BBC in the UK brought thirteen episodes and started airing them in August 1960. The British critics weren't quite as fond of the show as some of their American counterparts; the Daily Mirror noted that "Clumsy audience laughter, a stilted supporting cast and phoney accents hammered the show."[37] But some did enjoy it;

"Hiram Holliday is the sort of chap most undersized men would like to be. And as most men are undersized in one way or another, I'm sure that this little man of many parts will become a firm favourite on BBC TV.

Doubtless as his adventures progress we shall find that he has many more accomplishments—as many as the situations he's in require. For there's more than just a streak of fantasy in the exploits of Hiram Holliday.

He's the man Walter Mitty wanted to be. So extravagant, in fact, were some of last night's scenes that they were little more than a burlesque of this type of story.

But they were good fun, with Wally Cox making an excellent Hiram, with amusing dialogue and with one scene, the conclusion of the umbrella duel – suggesting a touch of comic genius.

Certainly Hiram's the best character to come out of an American can for a long, long time and that's saying something."[38]

---

37 3 August 1960
38 Liverpool Echo, 3 August 1960

And they must have been in the majority, for a few months after the initial airing the BBC repeated the show.

In Australia Hiram debuted at the end of 1960 initially airing on Sundays at 4.30pm but from early 1961 was switched to Saturdays at 6pm; a variety of channels across the country aired the show throughout the year. The show ran on TV Singapura—the first TV station in Singapore--as *Pengembaraan Hiram Holliday* in late 1968.

On August 25, 1967, NBC issued a distribution report for the show for the period ending June 30th of that year; the show had lost the network $353,388.39, even though it had earned $245,089 in cumulative sales ($69,271 domestic and $175,818 international).

An audio book was produced of the original collection of short stories. It was released in Australia in 1986, published by Hear a Book and read by Leon Waller. But it was Germany that was to prove perhaps the most interested in Hiram's adventures. It originally aired under the title of *Die seltsamen Abenteuer des Hiram Holliday* on ARD in the early 1960s and the first eleven episodes were rerun on Family TV in 2018. A DVD of those eleven episodes was released in 2013 and at the time of writing those episodes are also available on a well-known streaming platform, but sadly without an English language audio.

In April 1987 Paul Rapp, Joel's brother, received a letter from Dr Georg Feil, a writer and producer working for Bavaria Atelier, a German production company.

"As you have heard from our correspondent Lin Grayson of Cine Enterprises we are interested in producing a remake of the series 'Adventures of Hiram Holiday' as produced by your father. We are presently negotiating this project with one of the biggest West German television stations (Cologne). However in order to assess whether a production for the German market would be viable in 1987 we would be very happy if we could read the scripts."

Sadly nothing further came of this. However just a couple of years later[39] film industry trade paper *Variety* reported that:

"Indie producer William Allyn has added three new projects...He has also acquired the rights to Paul Gallico's novel "The Adventures of

---

39 8 June, 1989

Hiram Holliday", a story set in 1939 about an unassuming newspaper copy editor who vacations in Europe and who gets caught in international intrigue and fascism.

In the course of his adventure he becomes a great circus clown in France and a frontline reporter on the rising threat of Germany. "It's a splendid fable about a very sweet, very real hero, but with all the scope and adventure of an Indiana Jones story," said Allyn"

Allyn, who had spent several years as an Associate Producer on *Peyton Place* died in 1999 at the age of 71, without the project coming to fruition. That same year the show was being touted by Chatsworth TV Distributors, a UK company who made it available for sale at MIPCOM, however that also seems to have come to nothing.

Appendix 1: Pilot Script

THE ADVENTURES OF HIRAM HOLLIDAY

Written by
Philip Rapp

Based on the stories by Paul Gallico

FADE IN:
FULL SHOT - OCEAN LINER - DAY (STOCK)
A stunning shot of a huge luxury liner of the "Queen Elizabeth" type majestically ploughing through a placid ocean.

QUICK DISSOLVE
CLOSE SHOT - PORT BOW OF VESSEL (MOVING)
The name of the ship is revealed as "Britannique"
QUICK DISSOLVE
CLOSE SHOT - EMBROIDERED LETTERING "Britannique"
The CAMERA PULLS BACK to disclose the word is on the serving jacket of a deck steward. HE is bending over serving tea to somebody. OVER THE ACTION we HEAR the muffled SOUND of pistol shots.
WIDER ANGLE
To include a passenger in a deck chair. This is HAROLD STEVEN SHARPE, top trouble-shooter in the US Foreign Affairs Department, confidante of the President, and a man as well- known in the capitals of Europe as he is in Washington. His physical appearance reminds one of Dulles. He reaches for his cup of tea.

SHARPE
(frowning)
Where's the shooting, steward?

STEWARD
(foreign accent)
On the promenade deck, Excellency. Today is the finals in the passenger pistol competition...Sugar?

SHARPE
Thank you, no.

He holds the cup and saucer in his left hand. His righthand is hidden from view beneath his steamer blanket.

STEWARD
Permit me, Excellency, to wish you luck on your mission. All Europe prays for a satisfactory meeting.

SHARPE
We shall do our best steward. But we are prepared for any emergency.

STEWARD
My country has faith in your diplomacy, Excellency.

He bows slightly and moves on. The pistol shots can still be HEARD at intervals. The CAMERA MOVES in on Sharpe as he brings his right hand from under the blanket. A smallleather dispatch case is attached to his wrist by a handcuff. He shifts the cup and saucer to the manacled hand and raisesthe cup to his lips with the other. CAMERA remains on theleather case, which is stamped in goldletters:
HAROLD STEVEN SHARPE STATE DEPARTMENT
WIDER ANGLE
We become aware of a trench-coated figure a little to the left and behind Sharpe. He is a Secret Service man, Carson. Sharpe addresses him without turning.

SHARPE
(smiling)
I can always feel your presence, Carson. I think I shall come to no harm on this voyage.

CARSON
Thank you sir.

The pistol shots increase in tempo.
WIPE TO:

FULL SHOT SHOOTING GALLERY DAY
On the promenade deck. A group of people, consisting of mainly pretty girls and comely matrons, stand behind Major Spitalfield-Neves, who is completing his round of shots at a target with a .22 mounted on a .38 frame. The major, afamous adventurer-explorer-

soldier-of-fortune-big-game-hunter-writer sort of chap, over six feet tall. Dashing figure and piercing eyes, shoots with a flair and a flourish, performing to the admiration of all. He empties his pistol at the target, holsters it, and signals for the steward to reel in his card. As the attendant manipulates the line the target comes forward. It is unclipped and handed to the major. The girls crowd in for a look.

INSERT TARGET

None of the shots are out of the black and there are a fair percentage of bullseyes. Over the insert we HEAR the squeals of admiration from the girls.

MED SHOT MAJOR AND GROUP

MAJOR
(modestly)
Rather a pretty cluster for a rocking boat, what?
This gets a big laugh from the dames.

ATTENDANT
(looking at card)
Not bad, sir. Almost as good as Mr Holliday's.

MAJOR
Mr Holliday?

ATTENDANT
(producing another card)
Have a look, sir.

He hands him Holliday's target. Everybody leans in. INSERTS TARGET
It is signed "Hiram Holliday - N.Y." There is just onehole in it - right through the bullseye -- a trifle jagged perhaps, but only one hole.

BACK TO SCENE

MAJOR
There's only one hole!

ATTENDANT
Yes sir. One hole - ten bullets! Rather an unorthodox style Mr Holliday has - but he certainly gets the job done, I must say.

ONE OF THE GIRLS
Hiram Holliday? What a perfectly silly name!

MAJOR
(awed - still staring at the target)
This is fantastic

On the fringe of the group, jotting notes in a pad, stands a young man. His dress, his manner, his bearing, his look of tolerant resignation, all spells "reporter". We won't disappoint you. He is JOEL SMITH, roving reporter for the New York Sentinel.

MAJOR (CONT'D)
(shaking his head)
He must be the world's greatest marksman.

SMITH
(without looking up)
You don't know the half of it, brother!

DISSOLVE:

EXT. CORRIDOR - OUTSIDE SHIP'S HOSPITAL
A solemn group, including Major Spitalfield-Neves and some of the beauties seen earlier, press around a white-gowned surgeon. He still has his mask draped around his neck and wears the operating room cap.

MAJOR
(with superb simplicity)
If the patient needs a transfusion, doctor--

His gesture indicates that he will allow them to drain the last drop of blood from his body.

DOCTOR
Thank you, major – the crisis is past. She will recover.

GIRL
Was it a difficult operation?

DOCTOR
It's only been attempted twice before. Once by the celebrated surgeon Doctor Stuckerhof in Vienna and three years ago by our own Doctor Mayo. In both cases it was unsuccessful.

MAJOR
Then, doctor, you are to be thrice congratulated for a brilliant effort.

DOCTOR
1? I didn't perform the operation. It was done by Hiram Holliday.
Everybody reacts.

MAJOR
Hiram Holliday?

DOCTOR
Such technique! Such dexterity. And when you consider he accomplished it without any of the special instruments needed for the operation -- well!

There is a general expression of amazement from the group, while the Major keeps muttering "Hiram Holliday". The CAMERA PANS off to Joel Smith who leans against the wall taking in the entire scene.

SMITH
(to camera)
Without special instruments. That's a laugh. Hiram Holliday could perform a tracheotomy on a carpenter using the man's own brace and bit.

FULL SHOT - BELOW DECKS
DISSOLVE:
This is where the livestock is normally kept. On this voyage, however, most of the space is occupied by steel cages housing vicious jungle carnivores. The GROWLING and SNARLING of lions and tigers can be HEARD intermittently. The major and a group of people stand before one cage.
MED SHOT - GROUP
The major is holding forth.

MAJOR
Bad actor, this fellow.

CLOSE SHOT - LION IN CAGE
He snarls viciously and raises a murderous paw.

MAJOR'S VOICE (O.S.)
Decimated the population of the village of Nyanja in Africa.

MED SHOT - MAJOR AND GROUP
The girls are properly impressed.

GIRL
How did you ever take him alive, Major?

MAJOR
(waving it off)
All in a day's work.
(MORE)

MAJOR (CONT'D)
(moving off to another cage). Now here's a chap who gave me ---

There is a sudden commotion O.S. Everybody turns to look.

FULL SHOT - ENTRANCE TO BULKHEAD
A crewman, followed by other sailors and the ship's captain, enter the scene carrying a dismantled mechanical device. The crewman handles his burden gingerly as they pass through.

CAPTAIN
Up and over the side with it, men.
(stops and takes off his cap and mops his forehead)
Two thousand people - fifteen seconds from death

MAJOR
Good heavens! What was it, Captain?

CAPTAIN
A time bomb. Obviously designed to eliminate only one person.

MAJOR
Harold Steve Sharpe!

CAPTAIN
The President's personal envoy. (lowering his voice). If Mr Sharpe and the documents he is carrying never reach England - (he shrugs) -- I aged thirty years while the warhead on the infernal machine was being defused.

GIRL
It must have been terrifying

CAPTAIN
What an exhibition of skill and daring! Imagine disarming the time bomb with no equipment other than a shoe horn and a sail-maker's needle!

Pilot Script

MAJOR
(pointing off)
That young sailor? Where did he get the experience?

CAPTAIN
Sailor? Oh no. A passenger did it - Hiram Holliday.

MAJOR
(with a mixture of exasperation and amazement.
Who the devil is Hiram Holliday?

As the crowd echoes the question, the CAMERA MOVES over to the ever-present Joel Smith. He makes a few note sin hispad, then looks up.

SMITH
(directly to camera)
I suppose that's what everybody wants to know. Five days ago Hiram Holliday was an obscure proof reader for the New York Sentinel -- that's my paper too.

As his VOICE carries on, the scene DISSOLVES to:

FULL SHOT - NEWSPAPER OFFICE DAY (SILENT)
This is the copy room of the New York Sentinel. At a desk in the middle of the bustling office sits Hiram Holliday. The CAMERA MOVES in for a better look and it seems hardly worth it. Hiram Holliday is - well, if we assume that Major Spitalfield-Neves represents the dash, the physique, the looks of the perfect man, then Hiram is the other side of the coin. For one thing, his protective coloration practically removes him from sight. His small, roundish face, his ruffled sandy hair, his steel-rimmed spectacles, his remarkable tendency to assume a form of suspended animation, and his bland manner, plus his slightness of stature complete the picture of -- nothing.

SMITH'S VOICE (O.S)
There's Hiram Holliday. Best proof reader the Sentinel ever had.

Enveloped in reams of copy, Hiram's pencil fairly flies over the news stories, making a correction here, a deletion there, his eyes travelling over thousands of printed words with never a movement of his head.

SMITH'S VOICE (CONT'D)
Last week, just by transposing a misplaced comma, he saved the paper from a million dollar libel suit.

Hiram inserts a large comma.

SMITH'S VOICE (O.S.)(CONT'D)
Not much to look at, is he?
As Hiram scans the copy in front of him he inserts his long pencil in the sharpener attached to the desk and grinds away.

SMITH'S VOICE (O.S.) (CONT'D)
Actually, he's the most gifted man in the world. Secretly, and with infinite pains and patience Hiram has acquired all the outward attributes of the romantic hero.
The inner ones he always possessed.

Without looking up Hiram extracts his pencil from the sharpener. It is about a half inch long. He starts to work with it, realises what's happened, selects another one and continues.

SMITH'S VOICE (CONT'D)
For fifteen years he hoarded his salary and went to fencing salle and shooting school, took lessons in foil, epees, saber, pistol and rifle. He learned to ride, swing, box, ski and fly a plane. Always, eventually, this pupil outshone the master. And when he couldn't afford instruction he resorted to books, developing an encyclopedic knowledge embracing every art and skill, from surgery to savate.

During this Hiram is working steadily and rhythmically. Copy boys are handed finished copy by him without pause, nor does he look up as they approach and leave his desk. He is also filing copy in various baskets on his desk, and throwingsome in the wastepaper basket on the floor. On the final word "savate" he flips a ball of waste paper into the air and without a glance flips it with his heel into the wastebasket. SOUND now comes over the scene as the <u>angle widens</u> to include a glassed in office at the window of which stands Joel Smith and Harrison Prentice, the publisher.

MED SHOT INT. GLASSED OFFICE

SMITH
Nobody knows about these things except me, Mr Prentice, and I just found out yesterday.

PRENTICE
(staring off at Hiram)
Incredible! What a story!

SMITH
He dreams of being a gentleman adventurer

PRENTICE
On the contrary, Smith - we're the dreamers -- he's the realist. Come on.

They exit towards outer office.

CLOSE SHOT HOLLIDAY AT DESK
He's still working like a beaver. Smith and Prentice enter the scene. Hiram looks up, then rises.
GROUP SHOT - THE THREE

PRENTICE (CONT'D)
Holliday, I want you to know how grateful I am for your part in saving the paper from that libel suit.

HIRAM
(diffidently)
Any proof reader worth his salt would have done the same thing, Mr Prentice. After all, commas are a dime a dozen.

He gives a breathy little laugh.

PRENTICE
(staring at him)
Yes. Well here's something that'll buy you a lot of commas
(hands him a cheque)
This is a five thousand dollar bonus

HIRAM
(taking the cheque)
Well now, that's very nice of you

PRENTICE
And I'm promoting you to special reporter. Take a year, travel all over the world and send in stories. Expenses paid, of course.
Smith reacts but Hiram remains composed.

HIRAM
Oh? Mr Prentice, I'd like you to know that whilst I'm not given to outward emotional demonstrations my glands are pumping the adrenalin into my body at such an increased rate as to produce a most astonishing feeling of euphoria.

PRENTICE
What?

SMITH
(hastily)
What - er - What would you like to write about, Hiram? Abroad, I mean?

HIRAM
(cogitating)
Well -- numerous things, I suppose. If I could spend time in South America I might be able to write some dandy stuff on the suicidal impulses of the lemming.

PRENTICE
(still staring) Uh-huh

HIRAM
From England I could bring the reading public up to date on the interesting practice of "sagging the biscuit" - a method of producing bone china.

SMITH
(looking at Prentice)
That's a pretty good circulation getter.

HIRAM
The low countries will provide me with tons of material for a series on the sex life of the tulip.

PRENTICE
(rather stunned)
Yes. Take the rest of the day off, Holliday.

HIRAM
Thank you, sir.
He reaches into a drawer, pulls out a mackintosh, hat and furled umbrella, dons them and starts out. Prentice stares after him.

FULL SHOT OFFICE
Hiram reaches the fence separating the main office from a smaller reception office. There is an office boy, loaded with copy, coming through the swinging gate. Hiram steps to one side, plants his umbrella firmly on the floor using it as an assist while he vaults nimbly over the fence. He exits.

CLOSE SHOT PRENTICE AND SMITH

PRENTICE
Did you see that?

SMITH
I told you Mr Prentice,- he can do anything!

PRENTICE
Smith, I want you to stick with him wherever he goes. If you write the series properly, we'll triple our circulation.

SMITH
(startled)
Series! You want me to write about lemmings and tulips?

PRENTICE
No, you fool! Do the series on him! The Adventures of Hiram Holliday!

CLOSE SHOT SMITH
DISSOLVE:
In the same position as before the FLASHBACK - He puts away his notebook.

FADE IN:

SMITH
Well, that's it. Day after tomorrow around this time the ship will dock at Southampton. By then I can safely guarantee there won't be a single passenger on board who hasn't heard of Hiram Holliday.

FADE OUT:
FULL SHOT. PORTION OF DECK. DAY.
A fine, fog-like spray is in the air, a strong wind is blowing, and breasting it, clad in mackintosh and cap, clutching his furled umbrella, is Hiram Holliday. He comes forward and turns into a doorway.
CLOSE SHOT. DOOR.
It bears a sign - "GYMNASIUM". Hiram enters.
REVERSE ANGLE
As he comes through the door, closing it behind him.

FULL SHOT. GYM.
Typical gymnasium equipment. In the centre of the floor is a mat about forty feet long and six feet wide. This is a fencing pad. Foils, Protectors, drill jackets are hung about the walls. The gym instructor, Franz Dupree, a lithe graceful man in his middle thirties greets Hiram.

DUPREE
Bonjour, m'sieu.

HIRAM
(stripping off his coat, cap and laying aside his umbrella) Thank you. Bit drizzly out there this morning.

Dupree regards the little man quizzically as he meticulously hangs up his overcoat, folds his scarf, tucks it in his mackintosh pocket, then removes his jacket, hanging that up also. He wears no vest and his suspenders over his shirt give him a slightly comic look. Hiram turns and faces Dupree, gives a little sigh, then clasps his hands in front of him.

DUPREE
If I may be of service, m'sieu? You wish perhaps to work out with the dumbbells. To put on some -- muscle?

HIRAM
No. I thought possibly I might find somebody to fence with.

Although Hiram doesn't give the impression of much sport to come, Dupree bows graciously.

DUPREE
I shall consider it an honour, m'sieu. (he reached for a pair of foils). I am Franz Dupree, better known at the Brussels Academie de Fence as Le Flamand. It is rare that a fencer appears on the passenger list.

He hands Hiram a foil. The buttons at the tip are prominent and safe.

HIRAM
(declining it)
Would it be too much trouble if we used the epee?

DUPREE
(raising an eyebrow)
The epee, m'sieu? Avec le point d'arret?

HIRAM
Oui. It makes it more exciting - more like the real thing, you know?
(slowly) Oui.

DUPREE
He selects a pair of epees, each equipped with three short razor-sharpe prongs attached to the tip, hands one to Hiram. Hiram takes it, tests its flexibility tentatively. In the meantime, Dupree has donned the heavy canvas jacket, glove and mask.

DUPREE (CONT'D)
Your equipment, m'sieu.
He offers Hiram another canvas jacket, mask and glove.

HIRAM
Merci. But I prefer to fence as I am. That slows me down.
Dupree can't believe his ears.

DUPREE
But m'sieu -- the epee --

HIRAM
Don't be afraid.
Dupree stares at him a moment, then divests himself of all the safety equipment, flinging his mask and jacket to one side.

DUPREE
I will take the chance, m'sieu.

A grim smile plays over Dupree's mouth. He is obviously going to teach this clod a lesson. They both assume the *en garde* position. Dupree, deciding that this amateur must be quickly put in his place, devises a quick touch, a beat on the blade with a planned *pris-en-fer*. But somehow, Hiram's blade is not there to receive the beat! With magnificent grace, the lightness of thistledown and the speed of a gazelle, Hiram Holliday had suddenly become D'Artagnan at bay. Anticipating Dupree's move, Hiram drives forward with his weapon, pushing the attacking point outward, and in a series of lightening maneuvers bewilders his adversary with thrusts and parries, riposte, remise, counter-riposte and reprise and concluding with a crashing *balestra* and *rinverso tondo*. Unaccountable the great Flamand has been scored upon, and a dark red stain begins to appear through his shirt on his upper arm. Hiram drops his sword and rushes to him.

HIRAM
(with great concern)
I'm terribly sorry, I lost my head.

DUPREE
(staring at his arm) Magnifique! Formidable!

HIRAM
I have some bandaids in my cabin --

DUPREE
Non! Let it bleed. I shall wear this scar as a badge of honor.

HIRAM
(reaching for this things)
Well, if you're sure you're all right --

DUPREE
(with a little laugh)
It is my own fault. Next time, when I cross swords with such a blade as you, I wear the proper jacket, nein?

Hiram stands in his mackintosh, cap and carries his furled umbrella, once again the nondescript little man with the steel-rimmed glasses. He manages to get out of the gym, rather embarrassed under Dupree's admitting stare.

MED CLOSE SHOT - DUPREE

DUPREE (CONT'D)
(as Hiram leaves)
Magnifique! Incroyable!
(A sudden change of expression)
I will kill him for this!

FULL SHOT - GYM.
He dabs at his arm with a handkerchief. The door opens and the STEWARD, seen earlier on deck serving tea, enters. He acts in a stealthy manner and approaches Dupree with a conspiratorial air, CAMERA MOVING IN.

STEWARD
Listen, Franz –
(notices wound)
What happened?

DUPREE
(heavy sarcasm)
I cut myself shaving. How are things going?
They lower their voices to whispers.

STEWARD
Everything is arranged. Feodor is standing by.

DUPREE
And Marlene?

STEWARD
She knows her part. Once we have the dispatch case, you will proceed exactly according to plan.

DUPREE
The envoy suspects -- ?

STEWARD
Nothing. During the masquerade ball tonight a diversion will be created to return all passengers to their quarters. We shall strike precisely at midnight.

DUPREE
Midnight.

STEWARD
All that remains is the selection of a dupe. Marlene will attend to that.
And as he smiles smugly we
DISSOLVE:

INT. STATEROOM - NIGHT
Over the scene can be HEARD faintly the SOUND of orchestra music. This is the bedroom of Joel Smith. He is dressed as a swami and is just placing a jeweled turban on his head. He glances at himself in the mirror, nods, then goes to the door, CAMERA following. His door connects with a living room, which in turn connects with another bedroom. He reaches the bedroom door, knocks.

SMITH
(calling)
Hiram!

There is a BUZZING sound from the room. It stops at his second call. Hiram comes to the door, opens it. He is clad in his underwear and has a peculiar contraption in his hand to which is attached a long electric cord presumably plugged into a socket.

HIRAM
(admitting Smith's costume)
Say! That's just wonderful. You'll win a prize tonight for sure.
Smith is staring at the contraption in Hiram's hand.

SMITH
What's that thing?

HIRAM
This? Oh, it's just a little thing I made from a pair of thinning shears and the rotary blade of a cabbage slicer.

SMITH
What's it for?

HIRAM
I cut my hair with it…See?

He displays the back of his head. Smith stares.

HIRAM (CONT'D)
I hooked it up to a little three stage motor that I got out of an old barbecue.

SMITH
Why don't you go to a barbecue? I mean a barber?

HIRAM
I do sometimes. But when I'm in a hurry, like now, the old clippo comes in handy.

SMITH
I can see that.

HIRAM
I can shave with it too. And it's still good for slicing cabbages.

SMITH
A man ought to market a thing like that. Sweep the country.

HIRAM
Do you think so? Sometime I'll have to show you the scavenger pump I made for my lapidary wheel.

SMITH
Don't you forget now.

HIRAM
Oh I won't. Soon as we get back home.

During the foregoing, Hiram has been cutting his hair. He's done a rather uneven job.

SMITH
Have you got a costume for tonight?

HIRAM
Yes. It's just an old makeshift - I don't expect to win anything.

SMITH
(putting on a small mask)
Well, you might when you get done with that haircut. See you in the ballroom.

He goes. Hiram looks after him a moment, trying to figure out the last remark. He Shrugs and returns to his bedroom. The SOUND of music grows louder.

FULL SHOT. INT. BALLROOM NIGHT

Off to one side is an elaborate bar, thronged with costumed men and women. The dance floor is filled and an orchestra on a rostrum provides some lively music. Prominent are the Major, dressed as a cavalier, the ship's captain, in uniform, the ship's doctor, wearing a convict suit, and the envoy, in tails, dispatch case still attached to his wrist, accompanied by a uniformed policeman carrying a tommy gun. This is apparently Carson, the Secret Service man detailed to protect him. They all wear small masks.

ANOTHER ANGLE - TIGHTER

Dupree, masked, and in apache costume is conversing lightly with a beautiful woman, sheathed in the close-fitting skin of a cat. She is MARLENE. They are holding cocktail glasses, both empty. The DECK STEWARD, the accomplice, approaches them with a tray of drinks. They replace their empty glasses and take fresh ones. During this action we hear:

DUPREE
(sotto)
That is a real gun the policeman carries?

CLOSE SHOT ENVOY AND POLICEMAN
They appear to be enjoying the festivities.
THREE SHOT - DUPREE, STEWARD AND MARLENE
As they look off. The steward smiles.

STEWARD
It is not even a real policeman. The sharks have got the bodyguard a hundred miles back. That is Feodor.

MARLENE
(catching her breath)
Perfect. A perfect double.

STEWARD
The rendezvous with the plane is arranged. Be ready with the papers, Marlene.

Marlene's eyes are sweeping the room.

DUPREE
We have still not selected the dupe.

MARLENE
We have. Just now I have selected him.
They follow her gaze.

CLOSE SHOT AT ENTRANCE TO BALLROOM
Hiram Holliday stands framed in the drapes. He is made up as Mickey Mouse. He looks all around, beaming.
GROUP SHOT. THE THREE CONSIPRATORS
As they study him. The steward indicates satisfaction, moves out of scene.

MARLENE (CONT'D)
(ready to go to work)
Made to order.

She preens herself and starts forward to snare Hiram. Dupree, an odd look on his face, grasps her arm, detaining her.

DUPREE
Wait! That man -- he -- he seems familiar. I've seen him before.

MARLENE
I will be the one who is familiar, my dear Franz. He is already netted.

CLOSE SHOT HIRAM
Frankly staring at Marlene with the great admiration of a man for a beautiful woman.
TWO SHOT MARLENE AND DUPREE
Marlene is sending an enchanting smile in Hiram's direction.

DUPREE
(still worried)
I don't know. His walk -- that man, I swear I know him from somewhere.

But he is talking to himself. Marlene has already movedin for the kill.
MED SHOT HIRAM
He is returning Marlene's smile. She enters the scene. Hiram, slightly embarrassed, shifts uneasily.

MARLENE
(putting him at his ease)
I could not resist capturing my natural prey.

HIRAM
(looking at her costume, then his) I suppose it should be the other way around. I should be the catand you should be the mouse. Or if I'm a mouse you should be a piece of cheese.

MARLENE
You are naive. Woman is the huntress.

She takes his arm, and leads him towards the bar, CAMERA following.

HIRAM
Yes, I suppose so. Most philosophers seem to agree on that point...Are you - are you enjoying the trip?

MARLENE
Superb. I have a confession. This is my maiden voyage.
They are at the bar.

HIRAM
Well, I'm not married either. (she stares at him)
That's just a joke. I know what maiden voyage means.
(pause)
It isn't very funny.
(to bartender, suddenly)
Two horse's necks, please

The bartender reacts and goes to prepare the drinks.

MARLENE
(amused)
Horse's necks?

HIRAM
That's all I could think of. I won't drink mine, anyway. Alcohol causes a rash on my stomach.

The band has started a slinky tango. Marlene turns to Hiram, puts her face very close.

MARLENE
(softly)
Let's tango.

HIRAM
(uncertainly)
Well, I've never tried it. Of course, I have studied the basic steps as described by Velasquez –
(she has led him on to the floor)
-- in the original Spanish, and read a book or two on the Cuban Habanero, to which the tang is closely related --

They are dancing. Marlene is a beautiful dancer. Hiram, leading, is executing all the moves perfectly, but in the curious and stilted manner of one who has, as he says, learned it from a book. The effect is strangely comic. Other couples stop dancing to watch the oddly-matched pair. Growing more confident as he glides over the floor, Hiram lets out a notch or two. He is becoming master of the situation. As they dance past the bar, Joel Smith, with a pretty girl in tow, turns to look. When he sees it is Hiram he almost drops his drink.

CLOSE SHOT SMITH
Staring - open-mouthed.

SMITH
He never told me about that!

MED SHOT HIRAM AND MARLENE
By now he's got Valentino backed off the map. All he needs is the silk blouse, sash and gaucho boots. Unfortunately he looks like a cross between Hiram Holliday and Mickey Mouse. They glide out of the scene.
DISSOLVE:
INT. SHIP'S CORRIDOR NIGHT
(The band music is HEARD over the scene)
Approaching the door of a stateroom is the envoy, followed by the armed policeman. Sharpe lets himself into the cabin.
REVERSE ANGLE
As the policeman follows him in. He closes the door behind him. Sharpe turns to his bodyguard, holds his wrist up. He removes his mask.

SHARPE
It's all yours for the night, Carson.

The bodyguard produces a key, unlocks the cuffs and takes the dispatch case. Sharpe rubs his wrist and turns to remove his jacket.

CLOSE SHOT POLICEMAN.
An ugly look crosses his face. He raises his tommy gun and thrusts the butt forward violently. There is a dull thud.
MED SHOT BELOW DECKS - NIGHT
At the animal cages. The STEWARD enters in the semi-darkness, picking his way carefully over to the man-eating lion's cage. He clambers up on top, reaches down for a locking bar and pulls upward. There is a ROAR from the lion and he bounds from his prison.
FULL SHOT INT. BALLROOM
The music is loud and blaring, and the dancers are engaged in the "rock-and-roll." Most prominent, and most active, is Hiram Holliday and his partner Marlene. Marlene is performing well, but seems slightly distracted as if waiting for something to happen. It does. Suddenly over the public address system comes an urgent command.

VOICE
(filter)
Attention, everybody! Attention!

The music stops and the dancers come to a halt, look about wondering.

VOICE (CONT'D)
All passengers and personnel please immediately go to your quarters. There is no cause for panic, but a lion is loose below decks.

There is an immediate panic reaction from the passengers, who start to stream off.

VOICE (CONT'D)
Go immediately to your quarters. Will Major Spitalfield-Neves report at once to the bridge.

The girl is swept away from Hiram in the rush to get out of the ballroom. His glasses are knocked to the floor, and he gropes for them as the room empties.
CLOSE SHOT - HIRAM
He finally comes up with his glasses, gets them on and looks around.
FULL SHOT - BALLROOM
It is empty
CLOSE SHOT - HIRAM

HIRAM
Well, I guess I had better be getting along.

He starts out.

MED SHOT - SHIP'S CORRIDOR
It is deserted. Marlene comes around a passage. At the same moment, timed to perfection, a door opens, a hand holding the dispatch case is placed in her path. Without stopping she takes the small case and conceals it. She exits the scene.
MED SHOT - ANOTHER CORRIDOR

Hiram is walking briskly towards his stateroom. He opens the door to the living room and lets himself in.

FULL SHOT - LIVING ROOM
As he enters, a voice comes over the intercom.

VOICE
(filter)
Attention all passengers. Attention all passengers. Remain in your staterooms until further notice. As a safety precaution, lock all doors. Lock all doors.

Hiram locks the door.

VOICE (CONT'D)
(intercom)
Although every effort is being made, the lion is still at large.

Hiram makes a search of the room, looking under the couch then in more unlikely places. Finding nothing, he sits down in a chair, takes off the Mickey Mouse head and stares thoughtfully into space.
CLOSE SHOT - HIRAM

HIRAM
Well now.

There is suddenly a LOUD RAPPING on the door. He looks up.

MARLENE'S VOICE
(outside door)
Please! Let me in! Let me in! Help me!

WIDER ANGLE
Hiram goes to the door and opens it, and Marlene bursts in and throws herself into his arms, sobbing.

MARLENE
I...I lost my way...I can't find my cabin...I was terrified! Help me!
HIRAM
Gladly. I have a very good sense of direction.

He detaches himself and opens the door of the cabin, to lead her out. She reacts violently, hurling the door shot and arching her body against it.

MARLENE
No, no! I must stay here! Bolt the door!

HIRAM
You don't think we should leave it open?
Marlene points dramatically.

MARLENE
Death walks on four legs somewhere outside! Is this time for convention?

She bolts the door herself, then crosses toward the bedroom.

MARLENE (CONT'D)
(walking)
Pour me champagne...I have need of strong wine.

HIRAM
But I...
Marlene turns back to him, looking closely into his eyes.

MARLENE
Strong, heady wine.

She goes into the bedroom, closing the door behind her. Hiram looks after her a moment, then goes to the door to the corridor and opens it an inch or two. Obviously relieved he comes back and takes up the phone.

HIRAM
(into phone)
I suppose I wish to speak to the wine steward.

MED SHOT - BEDROOM
Marlene has quickly opened Hiram's luggage and is inserting the dispatch case in one of his bags.

CLOSE SHOT - HIRAM
He is seated, holding the phone.

HIRAM (CONT'D)
Hello? This is Hiram Holliday, Stateroom 506. I wonder if you're serving champagne while the lion is at large?

CRACKLING NOISES come from the receiver. Hiram is forced to hold it away from his ear whilst the NOISE persists, which is a considerable time. It finally subsides, and Hiram speaks into the phone. He nods that he has understood.

HIRAM (CONT'D)
No. Well, I should like to place an order for future delivery.

FULL SHOT - STATEROOM
Hiram is sitting with his back to the door. It opens slowly, and the man-eater, Simba, enters. Hiram is unaware of his presence.

VOICE
(filter)
The lion has been traced to B deck. Lock all doors!

HIRAM
(into phone) Excuse me.

He goes to the door and locks it, never seeing the lion. He returns to the phone.

HIRAM (CONT'D)
(into phone)
I would like champagne for one. As for myself, I believe I shall have a steak, New York, very rare, charcoal broiled. That's one steak.

As he is talking, the lion walks up behind him and thento his side. Hiram turns, and looks directly into the lions face.
TWO SHOT - HIRAM AND LION
Hiram turns back to the phone, then slowly turns and looks into the lions face again. He then speaks into the phone.

HIRAM (CONT'D)
You'd better make that two steaks.

FULL SHOT - STATEROOM
Marlene opens the door from the bedroom, and then freezes as she sees Simba. Hiram hangs up the phone and seeshei.

HIRAM (CONT'D)
I think we've captured the lion.

MARLENE
He's a killer!

HIRAM
(rising)
It is well-know that the so called King of the Beasts is in fact an arrant coward.

The lion growls menacingly.

HIRAM (CONT'D)
Pure bluster

MARLENE
Wh...what are you going to do?

Hiram crosses the room, followed by the lion.

HIRAM
The most effective weapon is neither spear not gun, but instead an ordinary chair. I shall cow him in seconds.

Hiram reaches the chair, and starts to pick it up by the back. Being on board ship, it is bolted to the floor. Hiram strains, then looks down.

CLOSE SHOT - CHAIR
It is seen that the legs are bolted down. The lion roars.

FULL SHOT - STATEROOM

HIRAM (CONT'D)
Well, now.

MARLENE
He'll kill us both!

HIRAM
Steady. I shall have to stare him down.

TWO SHOT - HIRAM AND LION
Hiram fixes the lion with an unblinking stare. The lion roars, and stretches out an angry paw. Hiram backs up slightly.

FULL SHOT - STATEROOM

HIRAM (CONT'D)
I may have to remove my glasses.

He takes off his glasses, then squints in the direction of the lion, who has moved around Hiram in the meantime. The lion roars again. Hiram turns.

HIRAM (CONT'D)
Oh. There you are.

The lion looks as if he is making ready to leap.

FULL SHOT - CORRIDOR
Major Spitalfield-Neves, with drawn pistol and whip, is coming cautiously down the corridor, followed at a little distance by fearful men with ropes and guns. They hear a LOUD ROAR from Hiram's cabin. All freeze in their tracks.

MAJOR
(gravely)
Too late. Simba has killed again.

He cautiously goes to the door of Hiram's cabin and suddenly throws it open, standing with gun at the ready.

FULL SHOT - STATEROOM (FROM DOORWAY)
The lion is sitting contentedly with his head in Hiram's lap, while Marlene watches, fascinated. Hiram looks up.

HIRAM
Come in gentlemen.

STATEROOM - ANOTHER ANGLE
The Major edges in, followed by the others.

MAJOR
Don't make a move, he's eaten 63 men!

HIRAM
(thoughtfully)
I think that was due to a vitamin deficiency

The Major cracks his whip at the lion.

MAJOR
Back, Simba! Back! Back!

The lion slowly goes to the door and out, with the Major and some of the men with guns following. Hiram stands up, plucking a lion's hair from his pants. By now, the ship's captain has entered the stateroom, and taken Hiram's hand in awe and admiration.

CAPTAIN
Sir, you are the bravest man I think I have ever seen.

HIRAM
It was nothing, really. Simply Semper Paratus.

CAPTAIN
Semper Paratus?

HIRAM
The Coast Guard motto. Always prepared. For such an emergency I always carry a spray of catnip.

The captain shakes his head.

CAPTAIN
Incredible. Incredible. Catnip.

HIRAM
Merely a sensible precaution, if you happen to be a mouse.

Marlene glides to his side, puts her feline arm around him, and gazes adoringly into his face. The captain steps back, to a position of attention.

CAPTAIN
Mr Holliday, I salute you...
(saluting)

And leave you to claim your reward

Hiram, somewhat startled, catches his meaning and looks at Marlene as the captain herds the others through the door and follows, closing it firmly behind him.

MARLENE
Hiram

He laughs nervously, and moves away slightly.

MARLENE (CONT'D)
Fearless before Simba, yet afraid of me?

HIRAM
(nervously)
Not really. It's just that I'm all out of catnip.

As she moves closer to him there is a LOUD KNOCK at the door. Hiram moves to it quickly and in relief, as if half-hoping Simba has returned. Hiram opens the door, and the steward enters quickly with a tray containing a bottle of champagne and glasses.

STEWARD
Compliments of the captain. The whole ship toasts your bravery.

He bows, closing the door behind him, then shows Hiram the champagne bottle.

STEWARD (CONT'D)
Remy-Frapin, '46

Hiram attempts a slight joke.

HIRAM
I'm N.Y.U, '43

The steward looks at him, then crosses to the bedroom to open the bottle.

MARLENE
He will pour the champagne. Sit with me, my hero.

She pulls him down to the chair, then sits at his knee. She steals a glance into the bedroom through the open door.

BEDROOM - MARLENE'S P.O.V

The steward looks out and catches Marlene's eye. He puts something into Hiram's glass, then opens the champagne bottle.

MED SHOT - STATEROOM

Hiram is sitting rather stiffly.

HIRAM
(to Marlene)
Perhaps we should attempt to find your stateroom.

Marlene merely looks at him.

MARLENE
So brave, so timid.

The steward comes in with two filled glasses. He presents one to Marlene, the other to Hiram.

STEWARD
Madame...Monsieur.

HIRAM
No, thank you. But I would appreciate a steak.

Marlene takes Hiram's glass from the tray and forces it on him.

MARLENE
Drink! You do not like champagne?

HIRAM
(considering)
I don't know...I never tried it.

She clinks glasses.

MARLENE
Drink! And you shall never be the same man.

HIRAM
Say! That sounds interesting.

He drains his glass at a gulp, as Marlene and the steward watch him. She waves the steward out, and he goes, looking back at Hiram.
TWO SHOT - HIRAM AND MARLENE
She watches him closely for a reaction. He gazes into space then hiccups slightly.

MARLENE
Can I get you more champagne?

HIRAM
(slowly, into space)
I think I should like another lion.

WIPE TO:
FULL SHOT - SHIP'S BRIDGE - NIGHT
The captain is in command as Mr Sharpe suddenly bursts onto the scene, in great agitation. He is disheveled and has a bandage round his head.

SHARPE
Captain! Captain!

The Captain goes quickly to him.

CAPTAIN
Mr Sharpe? What's the matter?

SHARPE
Get me Washington on the phone...the White House!

CAPTAIN
The White House? At three in the morning?

SHARPE
Don't waste time, man! Do it!

The captain turns to his radio operator.

CAPTAIN
The White House

The radio operator starts to make the contact, and the captain turns back to Sharpe

CAPTAIN (CONT'D)
Who at the White House, sir?

SHARPE
I will talk with only one man...The Chief.

RADIO OPERATOR
(to captain)
Contact established, sir.

SHARPE
(to captain)
Clear the bridge.

CAPTAIN
But...

SHARPE
Now.

The captain turns to the others.

CAPTAIN
Clear the bridge

The others exit, and Sharpe picks up the radio phone, waiting until all have left except the captain.

SHARPE
(into phone)
Chief? Sharpe here. Sir, the dispatch case has been stolen.

The captain reacts. Sharpe listens on the phone.

SHARPE (CONT'D)
Yes sir. Yes sir. I...I understand, sir.

He hangs up.

CAPTAIN
But how did such a thing happen? How? Who did it?

SHARPE
They will never reach shore with that case. Never. Planes are on their way.

FULL SHOT – HIRAM'S ROOM - MORNING

MARLENE
Good morning darling.

Hiram quickly paws his night table beside the bed for his glasses, finally finds them, puts them on, and looks at his bed partner.

MARLENE (CONT'D)
How do you feel, my dearest one?

HIRAM
I feel that events have occurred of which I am substantially unaware.

MARLENE
You don't remember? What you have missed.

HIRAM
Perhaps if you'd give me your name a slight bell would sound.

MARLENE
And what is your name?

HIRAM
Hiram Holliday.

MARLENE
I'm Mrs Hiram Holliday.

HIRAM
Really? I have a mother by the same name.

MARLENE
And a wife.

HIRAM
I think I shall consider that humour.

He laughs, but it has a hollow ring. He then gets quickly out of bed, is embarrassed to find himself in pajamas, and hastily gets into his robe. Marlene watches him, amused. He turns to her.

HIRAM (CONT'D)
Now, then.

MARLENE
You don't remember? We were married by the captain...after you drank the champagne

She throws back the sheet and prepares to get up.

HIRAM
(quickly)
Don't get up!

MARLENE
Why not?

HIRAM
I see your costume of last night...and it is not on you. It was an inadequate cover at best.

MARLENE
(getting up)
Don't be silly, darling.

She gets out of bed wearing a nightgown. She slips on a robe, then comes over to him.

MARLENE (CONT'D)
You really don't remember... how you swept me off my feet?

HIRAM
In a word, no.

MARLENE
What passion...what fire...

HIRAM
I wish I had been there.

MARLENE
Darling...you do believe me? How can we start off our marriage without trust?

HIRAM
Madame, I am afraid we are about to have our first altercation.

They both turn to a porthole at the SOUND of an approaching plane.

FULL SHOT - BRIDGE - DAY
The captain is using a pair of binoculars, looking at an object approaching the ship. Sharpe stands anxiously by him.

SHARPE
It is our plane, Captain?

Without answering him, the captain turns to the radioman.

CAPTAIN
Signal him again.

RADIO MAN
(excitedly)
He won't answer, sir! He won't respond!

The captain turns gravely to Sharpe.

CAPTAIN
Mr Sharpe, the plane is one of theirs.

LONG SHOT - PLANE LANDING ON WATER (STOCK)
FULL SHOT -BRIDGE
The captain takes down his binoculars and turns to Sharpe.

CAPTAIN (CONT'D)
Whoever they are, they've got nerve. No one can get off this ship...it's doing thirty knots.

SHARPE
(excitedly)
Thirty knots? Captain...we're losing speed.

The captain leaps to the engine control.

CAPTAIN
Who ordered reduced speed?

MATE
No one, sir!

CAPTAIN
Ring the engineer room!

The mate attempts to ring, but the controls do not answer.

MATE
Engineer room doesn't answer, sir!

CAPTAIN
They must!

The captain springs to the controls, but gets no response.

SHARPE
What is it? What does it mean?

The captain stares at him.

CAPTAIN
I don't know...I don't know!

FULL SHOT - HIRAM'S STATEROOM - DAY
Marlene is looking out the porthole at the plane as Hiram sniffs his champagne glass of the night before.

HIRAM
I detect the telltale odor of pyrobentathon

Marlene turns from the porthole.

MARLENE
Well?

HIRAM
Since that is not a usual ingredient of champagne I can only assume that I was drugged.

MARLENE
(calmly)
Of course

HIRAM
It's quite a relief. Nothing personal, but I would rather be drugged than married. You wanted a safe place for the dispatch case.

MARLENE
And we found one

HIRAM
In my bag. I have it.

He produces the case from inside his robe. Marlene starts forward

HIRAM (CONT'D)
I am afraid you may spend our honeymoon in jail.

As he is standing with his back to the door, it opens silently and Dupree glides in, followed by the steward. Dupree holds a drawn rapier, which he presses against Hiram's back.

DUPREE
Monsieur Holliday. The dispatch case...our plane has arrived...No. Do not turn around.

CLOSE SHOT - HIRAM
His features betray no fear, and his eyes become a alive with a plan. He spots his furled umbrella hanging within easy reach.
GROUP SHOT.
Marlene has come around in front of Hiram. Hiram shrugs, makes as if to hand the case to Dupree, then suddenly darts his other hand towards the umbrella. He is now armed. Retaining the case in his left hand he wields the umbrella against Dupree, the shining ferrule becoming an unpleasant and dangerous weapon. Taken completely by surprise, Dupree is thrown off guard and Hiram now has the position at the door, with a swift circling manouevre. The strange duel, fought in complete silence, is carried into the corridor, and up a narrow flight of stairs, with Dupree pressing forward and Hiram yielding inch by inch. During the fight Hiram manages to get a thrust toward the steward, dislodging a fronttooth, and when a small calibre pistol is produced by Marlene, he employs a savate kick to rid her ofit.

MED SHOT - DECK - TOP OF STAIRWAY

Hiram is forced out onto the open deck, with Dupree pressing after him. They fight their way across deck and Hiram is acquitting himself well when he trips over a capstan and stumbles backward against the rail. Dupree sees his advantage and comes forward in a tremendous thrust for the kill. Hiram is holding his umbrella in both hands, in an impossible position. As Dupree is upon him, the umbrella opens, and Dupree goes up and over the rail in a perfect and amazed swan dive. Hiram gets to his feet and looks over the side, closing his umbrella and giving the departed Dupree the fencer's salute.

FULL SHOT - DECK

Hiram is joined at the rail by a group of passengers in their robes, who have been roused by the excitement. Sharpe and the Captain come hurrying up, and a group of sailors follow with a firm grip on the disabled steward and Marlene. Also in irons is Feodor, the imposter.

HIRAM

I believe this is yours, Mr Sharpe.

He picks up the dispatch case and hands it to Sharpe who quickly checks the contents, then turns gratefully to Hiram.

SHARPE

Your country owes you a debt it can never repay, sir.

The major comes charging into the scene, Webley-Vickers in hand, running second as usual.

MAJOR

(out of breath)
Can I be of service, Sir?

Obviously he cannot.

SHARPE

(to major)
Thank you, no. The situation is well in hand, thanks to Mr Hiram Holliday.

The Major stares in open-mouthed admiration at Hiram

MAJOR
You are Hiram Holliday?

HIRAM
Yes, sir.

MAJOR
The man who bested me on the target range, who shot ten bulls on a rocking boat?

Hiram puts a hand to the rail, swaying slightly.

HIRAM
Rocking boat?

MAJOR
The man who performed that operation, who dismantled the time bomb? Who out-fenced Flamand? Who subdued Simba?

HIRAM
Catnip.

The Major ignores this.

MAJOR
And now you have single-handedly put down the world's most dangerous spy ring? You are the most magnificent fighting machine I ever encountered.

HIRAM
Thank you.

MAJOR
Hiram Holliday, I salute you. No man, no force in the world can ruffle the calm, cool daring of your...

He breaks off as Hiram lets go of the rail and starts uncertainly across the deck.

HIRAM
Excuse me.

MAJOR
Where are you going?

HIRAM
To my cabin. I believe I need some dramamine.

All stare at him as he wobbles with, with his umbrella.

DISSOLVE:

INT. HIRAM'S STATEROOM - DAY

Hiram is in the act of swallowing some tablets. He now removes his robe and prepares to lie down in bed. Joel Smith enters in street clothes from the living room, yawning.

SMITH
Are you just going to bed?

HIRAM
Well, I thought I'd sort of lie down for a little while.

SMITH
(a knowing smile)
You dog. You must have had some night. That brunette you were dancing with was certainly some witch!

HIRAM
Wasn't she?

SMITH
I couldn't hold out after eleven-thirty. Slept like a log. Anything happen?

Pilot Script

HIRAM
Oh yes. Very exciting.

SMITH
(perking up)
What? What was it?

HIRAM
I won fourth prize at the costume ball.
Smith shakes his head in a hopeless gesture as Hiram turns over on his side and goes to sleep.

FADE OUT:

THE END

NOTE: A series of incidents, highlights of future episodes, involving Hiram Holliday in dramatic and comic situations can be appended to the pilot, all narrated by Smith and giving part of the plot, depending on time and budget allowance.

Appendix Two: The Adventure of the Treasure Trove

FADE IN:

EXT. YACHT - DAY - FULL SHOT - (STOCK)

A luxurious yacht. SUPERED over the SHOT are the words, "Somewhere in the Pacific"

DISSOLVE TO:

EXT. DECK - DAY - MED. SHOT - GROUP

HIRAM, GARREAUX, and MARLENE. Hiram is dressed in bathing trunks and a diver's face mask and is being handcuffed and chained by Garreaux. Also visible on the deck is a chest, approximately large enough to uncomfortably quarter one small man. Garreaux finishes attaching the handcuffs, and then begins to wrap a heavy chain around Hiram.

GARREAUX
Soon it will be over, eh Hiram Holliday?

HIRAM
(glancing at the chains and the chest)
Unless you have a sudden change of heart, yes.

GARREAUX
(smiling)
A change of heart? How can that be-- when no heart exists?

HIRAM
Now, Garreaux. I've always found you to be most sentimental.

GARREAUX
(considering it)
Yes, I am sentimental.

MARLENE
(warningly)
Garreaux...

GARREAUX
(back to work)
But you have interfered for the last time.

HIRAM
(nodding)
I have been a bother, haven't I?

GARREAUX
Yes. Every time I was about to become the most powerful man in the world, what happened?

HIRAM
I came along to spoil it

GARREAUX
Yes. Remember, Hiram Holliday, in Paris -- the circus --?

HIRAM
(smiling) Yes indeed

OIL DISSOLVE TO:

INT. - CIRCUS - DAY - FULL SHOT - (HIRAMSTOCK)
(PLAY SEQUENCE FROM "ADVENTURE OF THE HOLLOW UMBRELLA" WHICH WILL INCLUDE AERIAL EXHIBITION BY HIRAM AND REACTION CUTSOF GARREAUX AND MARLENE)

DISSOLVE BACK
TO:

EXT. DECK - DAY - MED. SHOT - GROUP

As before. Garreaux is still chaining Hiram, albeit now with a far-away look in his eyes.

GARREAUX
It was fun, wasn't it!

HIRAM
I enjoyed it, yes.

GARREAUX
Do you recall Monte Carlo?

HIRAM
(nodding)
The ballet? I'm afraid I was less than adequate.

GARREAUX
You were superb! Such classic grace...such deep feeling...

OIL DISSOLVE TO:

INT. BALLET - NIGHT - MED SHOT - (HIRAM STOCK)

As Hiram comes from the wings at the end of the row of the dancers.
(PLAY BITS OF THIS SEQUENCE TO INCLUDE REACTION CUTS OF GARREAUX)

DISSOLVE BACK
TO:

EXT. DECK - DAY - MED. SHOT - GROUP

As before.

HIRAM
(beaming)
The Spectre of the Rose.

GARREAUX
You made it bloom like an orchid (a slight pause, then:)
Do you remember the opera?

HIRAM
Yes. When I hypnotized you.

GARREAUX
(going glassy)
Yes. When you hypnotized me.

MARLENE
(growing uneasy)
Garreaux, please...

GARREAUX
(not hearing)
It was magnificent...

OIL DISSOLVE TO:

INT. OPERA (DRESSING ROOM) - NIGHT - MED SHOT - HIRAM AND GARREAUX (HIRAM STOCK)

HIRAM
I suggest that you are not happy with your identity...you seek out another.

GARREAUX
I am not happy

HIRAM
You would be much happier as someone else.

GARREAUX
I would be much happier as someone else...

HIRAM
You would be much happier as Hiram Holliday...

DISSOLVE BACK
TO:

EXT. DECK - DAY - MED. SHOT - GROUP

As before

GARREAUX
I am happier! I am Hiram Holliday.

Quickly Marlene moves to Garreaux's side and slaps his face. He shakes his head and looks about, uncertain.

MARLENE
Garreaux, stop it!

GARREAUX
Why do you hit me, Marlene? I was so happy...

MARLENE
Finish your business. The submarine will soon be here.

GARREAUX
Yes. The submarine which will pick up the plans I have so carefully obtained.

HIRAM
I couldn't drop them off for you? On my way down?

GARREAUX
Thank you, no. You will step into the chest, please.

Hiram complies.

HIRAM
I guess one might say you were "packing me in".

He laughs it up as Garreaux smiles.

GARREAUX
At last I am to become the most powerful man in the world. You are not uncomfortable?

HIRAM
Not really. But as they say, it's not the Waldorf.

Garreaux draws a huge lock from his pocket.

GARREAUX
I shall now close the chest and lock it.

MARLENE
Hurry, Garreaux!

He slams down the top of the chest and snaps the lock into place.

GARREAUX
There! My treasure! Is it not fitting?

MARLENE
It is fitting. Push it overboard.

GARREAUX
(calls into chest)
You cannot get out?

There is the SOUND of muffled thumping from within the chest.

HIRAM'S VOICE
(muffled)
No, I'm afraid not.

GARREAUX
Good

He pushes the chest to the rail, hesitates for a brief, sad moment, then pushes it into the sea.

GARREAUX
(continuing)
Hiram Holliday, hail and farewell!

ANOTHER ANGLE

As Garreaux's face loses its triumphant smile and instead becomes hurt and remorseful.

MARLENE
You have done it, at last!

GARREAUX
(sadly) Yes. I know.

MARLENE
You are not happy?

GARREAUX
I am miserable

MARLENE
You are happy. Happy, happy, happy!

GARREAUX
No. I am filled with a sadness...a longing for him to be alive...

MARLENE
He has caused you nothing but trouble. Now he ahs gone.

She looks over the rail.

MARLENE
(continuing)
He is far away. Down there.

Garreaux moves to the rail and looks down.

GARREAUX
Yes, he is there. I shall bring him back!

Garreaux starts to remove his coat, preparatory to diving in after Hiram. Marlene slaps him again.

MARLENE
Garreaux!

GARREAUX
(snapping out)
Why am I standing here? I might fall into the water!

He makes his characteristic exit, as Marlene shakes her head and moves out after him.

EXT. CABIN DOOR - DAY - MEDIUM SHOT - GARREAUX AND MARLENE

As they move to the door and open it.

INT. CABIN - DAY - FULL SHOT

JOEL is seated in the room. He rises as Garreaux and Marlene enter.

GARREAUX
It is done, M'sieu Smith.

JOEL
It's impossible! You couldn't kill Hiram.

GARREAUX
No?
(he indicates Marlene)
My witness.

JOEL
Is it true?

MARLENE
It is true.

Joel sinks into a chair, head in hands.

JOEL
I can't believe it...

GARREAUX
It is difficult, yes.

JOEL
He was the best friend I ever had.

GARREAUX
Yes. I also.

JOEL
It seems like yesterday that we arrived in Tahiti and all this started...

OIL DISSOLVE TO:

EXT. ISLAND - DAY - FULL SHOT - (STOCK - FROM AIR)

DISSOLVE TO:

EXT. SIDE OF BOAT - DAY - FULL SHOT - SIGN

It reads: "The Tahitian - Dive for Sunken Treasure. Daily and Weekly Rates."

CUT TO:

EXT. DECK - DAY - MED SHOT - HIRAM AND JOEL

Standing on the deck of a small craft. Hiram is being helped into a regulation diving suit by a Polynesian NATIVE as Joel looks on, eating a native dish.

JOEL
Hiram, this is ridiculous.

HIRAM
Not so, Joel. I find the prospect most stimulating.

JOEL
I mean, how can you fall for a phony gag like this? It's strictly for the tourists.

HIRAM
Perhaps, Joel. But you will admit that we're not exactly natives.

JOEL
Sunken treasure! That's a laugh.

HIRAM
According to authorities, Joel, these waters abound with sunken riches.

JOEL
Authorities! The Tahiti Chamber of Commerce and the Organised Boat Owners Society!

HIRAM
You'll see Joel. I fully intend to bring back a chest of gold.

JOEL
You do that. If you need any help, let me know.

The native boy slips the diving helmet over Hiram's head, and Hiram clumps to the rail and slips into the sea below.

STOCK SHOT - DIVER

As he sinks into the water ANOTHER STOCK SHOT - DIVER
As he moves along the ocean floor, searching. CLOSE SHOT - HIRAM
SHOOTING THROUGH plate glass in helmet. His bespectacled eyes search the deep.

The Adventure of the Treasure Trove

MED SHOT - OCTOPUS

A few feet from Hiram CLOSE SHOT - HIRAM

He does not see the octopus, but he reacts to something else o.s

POV SHOT - THE CHEST

Nestled in a distinctive coral formation

WIDE ANGLE - (STOCK)

As the diver moves toward the chest. He reaches the chest, when the octopus suddenly appears in the shot and entangles the diver in his tentacles.

CLOSE SHOT - HIRAM

As he reacts. Pieces of tentacle are seen in the shot.

STOCK SHOT - DIVER

Fighting the octopus. He finally subdues it, and as the octopus floats off, the diver picks up the chest.

MED SHOT - HIRAM

With the chest in his arms

STOCK SHOT - DIVER
Rising toward the surface
STOCK SHOT - DIVER

As he surfaces alongside an appropriate boat

EXT. DECK - DAY - MED. SHOT - JOEL ANDNATIVE

As they pull Hiram aboard. The native quickly takes off Hiram's helmet.

HIRAM
Well I didn't need any help after all. With the chest, that is.

JOEL
(wide-eyed)
Hiram! You found one!

HIRAM
Naturally

JOEL
What's in it?

HIRAM
I don't really know. Although I suspect it might contain something useful to an octopus.

JOEL
What?

HIRAM
I encountered one down below.
(before Joel can reply)
Say. This is interesting.

JOEL
Huh?

HIRAM
This lock. It appears to be brand new!

JOEL
Really?

HIRAM
(nods)
And this chest bears the name of Tahiti's largest department store.

JOEL
I get it! Advertising!

HIRAM
Advertising?

JOEL
Sure. The department store plants the chests, and this boat leads you to them. A gimmick.

HIRAM
Perhaps. But they neglected to include a key.

JOEL
Let's get off this barge and back to the hotel. We can open it there.

HIRAM
All right.

He slips out of the suit and the native carries it away. Joel and Hiram start out of the shot when Joel stops.

JOEL
Did you say something about an octopus Hiram?

HIRAM
It was nothing Joel. Let's go.

DISSOLVE TO:

EXT. HOTEL - DAY - FULL SHOT - (STOCK)

Tahiti's finest.

DISSOLVE TO:

INT. HOTEL ROOM - DAY - MED SHOT - HIRAM AND JOEL

Hiram is working on the lock.

JOEL
How's it coming?

HIRAM
Almost, Joel.

He works a moment more, then clicks the lock open. Slowly he opens the chest as Joel looks on with great anticipation.

HIRAM (CONT'D)
(continuing)
Well now.

INSERT - CHEST

It is totally empty.

MED. SHOT - HIRAM AND JOEL

JOEL
How do you like that!

HIRAM
It's <u>different</u>, Joel. A treasureless chest.

JOEL
Sure. Remind me to shop at that department store.

Joel turns away, but Hiram peers closer into the chest, puts his hand inside and reacts.

HIRAM
Don't declare your boycott yet, Joel.

JOEL
Huh?

HIRAM
(pulls out a strip of wood)
False bottom.

JOEL
Hey...

Hiram now pulls some papers out of the chest and reads them.

HIRAM
I believe, Joel, that we have discovered something of greater value than buried treasure.

JOEL
Let me see!

Joel takes the papers and reacts.

HIRAM
I rather doubt they were left by the department store.

JOEL
These papers in the wrong hands...it would be disastrous!

HIRAM
You're quite right. I suggest we get them to the territorial Police Chief at once

JOEL
Come on!

They start out.

QUICK DISSOLVE TO:

EXT. POLICE CHIEF'S DOOR - DAY - MED. CLOSE SHOT.

The lettering reads: "Louis Nuveau, Territorial Police Chief."

DISSOLVE THROUGH TO:

INT. NUVEAU'S OFFICE - DAY - MED SHOT - NUVEAU

Seated behind his desk, a corpulent, perspiring Frenchman, who is mopping his face with his handkerchief. A colorful parrot is standing on his desk, preening.

NUVEAU
Everything is ready, my friend.

The CAMERA PULLS BACK to reveal Garreaux and Marlene in the room.

GARREAUX
Good.

NUVEAU
The money. You brought it with you?

PARROT
(with a French accent) The money, the money.

NUVEAU
(to the bird) Silence Gaugin!

GARREAUX
(with a look at the parrot)
I brought the money

Garreaux pulls out a wad of money and hands it to Nuveau.

NUVEAU
It is all here?

GARREAUX
It is all there. Where are the papers?

NUVEAU
Hidden in the sea.

GARREAUX
What?

NUVEAU
I am the Chief of Police, Garreaux! It is necessary that I take every precaution.

GARREAUX
Of course. Where are they hidden?

NUVEAU
In a chest. Here is a map showing the location. And here is the key.

He hands Garreaux the map and the key.

GARREAUX
(looking at the key)
They key to the world, Marlene.

MARLENE
Unless something should go wrong. Or <u>someone</u> should interfere.

Garreaux reacts, frightened.

GARREAUX
You have seen him?

MARLENE
No.

GARREAUX
Of course not. He is far away. That is why I chose to operate here.

NUVEAU
You must leave here, Garreaux. It would not be good for me to be seen with you.

PARROT
Leave, leave.

GARREAUX
Someday, Nuveau, I shall be hungry and I shall enjoy every bite of that bird!

PARROT
Get out, get out!

Garreaux glares at the bird, then smiles at the key.

GARREAUX
Come, Marlene.

They move to the door and exit.

INT. CORRIDOR - DAY - MED SHOT - GARREAUX AND MARLENE

As they exit Nuveau's office and start down the hall. They round a corner and just as they disappear from sight, Hiram and Joel appear at the other end of the hall and move to Nuveau's door.

HIRAM
This is it, Joel.

Hiram and Joel enter the door. There is a slight pause, and Garreaux suddenly appears, wide-eyed, at the end of the hall where he has just disappeared.

Garreaux is joined by Marlene.

MARLENE
What is it?

GARREAUX
He is here!

MARLENE
He is not here! He is far away!

GARREAUX
I heard him. I know I did.

MARLENE
You always hear him! Everywhere!

GARREAUX
You did not hear him?

MARLENE
Hiram Holliday cannot interfere with this plan. Now come!

GARREAUX
Yes. I shall come. I must find my sunken treasure.

He exits as we

FADE OUT:
END OF ACT ONE

FADE IN:

INT. NUVEAU'S OFFICE - DAY - MED SHOT - HIRAM AND JOEL

As they stand before Nuveau's desk. The parrot is still pacing his corner.

NUVEAU
May I help you, gentlemen?

HIRAM
I believe you might. My name is Hiram Holliday. This is my associate, Joel Smith.

PARROT
Hiram Holliday. Joel Smith.

HIRAM
Say, he is clever.
(to the bird)
Comment-allez vous?

PARROT
(excited)
Hiram Holliday, Hiram Holliday.

NUVEAU
Your business, M'sieu Holliday?

HIRAM
(hands Nuveau the papers)
I believe these will be self- explanatory

Nuveau looks at the papers and reacts.

NUVEAU
Where did you get these?

JOEL
In a treasure chest!

NUVEAU
Incroyable! A one-in-a-million chance...

HIRAM
Approximately. As you can see, these papers are most important to the security of the Pacific.

NUVEAU
Yes, I see. Rest assured, Messieurs, they will now be properly cared for.

JOEL
Good. Thanks Chief.

NUVEAU
Not at all. Au 'voir M'sieu Smith, M'sieu Holliday.

PARROT
Hiram Holliday, Hiram Holliday

HIRAM
Good day
(to the parrot) Au 'voir

PARROT
Hiram Holliday, Hiram Holliday

Hiram and Joel exit, and Nuveau rises, pacing nervously.

EXT. CORRIDOR - DAY - MED SHOT - HIRAM AND JOEL
As they exit Nuveau's office and move down the hall, the CAMERA FOLLOWING THEM. From around another corner come Garreaux and Marlene, and while Hiram and Joel are engaged in some unheard conversation, Garreaux and Marlene walk right by them to Nuveau's door, this time the CAMERA FOLLOWING THEM.

MARLENE
Garreaux! Did you see?

GARREAUX
(at the door)
See what?

MARLENE
Those two men...

GARREAUX
What about them?

MARLENE
It was Hiram Holliday and his friend!

GARREAUX
What?? Now you too see Hiram Holliday?
(he suddenly softens)
But I understand. He has a certain attraction...I am not angry with you Marlene.

MARLENE
Garreaux, I know what I saw!

GARREAUX
Of course, Marlene. Come. We must deal with the lying policeman.

He pushes open the door and he and Marlene enter the office.

INT. OFFICE - DAY - FULL SHOT

As Garreaux and Marlene enter. Nuveau reacts, as Garreaux moves to his side, gun drawn.

NUVEAU
Garreaux! I am glad you are here!

GARREAUX
Are you, my friend?

NUVEAU
Oui. I have the plans!

GARREAUX
Of course. And also my money.

NUVEAU
You don't understand, Garreaux...

GARREAUX
Please. My diver is most competent. Had there been a chest, he would have found it.

NUVEAU
But there was a chest...

GARREAUX
Of course. My money, please. And the plans.

NUVEAU
But...

GARREAUX
Quickly!

Nuveau hands Garreaux the money and the plans.
CLOSE SHOT - GARREAUX

GARREAUX (CONT'D)
(continuing)
Thank you, my friend. And now -- your reward.

He fires at the o.s Nuveau.

ANOTHER ANGLE

As Garreaux delicately blows the smoke from the barrel of his gun and replaces it. (we do not, in this ANGLE, see Nuveau in the shot.) The parrot is pacing the desk, frightened.

GARREAUX (CONT'D)
(continuing)
Come, Marlene. To the yacht

They start out, just as the parrot begins to chatter excitedly.

PARROT
Hiram Holliday, Hiram Holliday.

Garreaux freezes.

GARREAUX
Marlene. Did you hear him?

MARLENE
Yes. He said it.

GARREAUX
The bird hates me. He is exacting his revenge.

MARLENE
No! Holliday was here! I saw him.

GARREAUX
Yes. Then it must have been he who found the plans, and brought them to Nuveau.

MARLENE
Of course.

They exit.

(a pause)
What are you going to do?

GARREAUX
Find Hiram Holliday. Come.

DISSOLVE TO:

INT. HOTEL - DAY - TWO SHOT - HIRAM AND JOEL

Hiram is reading from a book as Joel munches on a sandwich. Hiram is dressed for the beach, as is Joel.

JOEL
Hiram, will you come on? We're missing the best part of the day!

HIRAM
In a moment, Joel. As soon as I finish this chapter on Hippospongia Maeandriformis, or Caribbean Turkey Sponge!

Joel begins to pace, when there is a KNOCK on the door. Joel moves to the door and opens it, revealing Garreaux and Marlene, Garreaux with gun drawn. Before Joel can move, Garreaux and Marlene are in the room and the door isclosed.

GARREAUX
So. We meet again.

JOEL
Garreaux! Marlene!

HIRAM
(noting the gun)
It is apparent that our meeting was not entirely accidental.

GARREAUX
I have travelled the globe searching for you, Hiram Holliday.

HIRAM
Thank you.

GARREAUX
This time, you will not escape the vengeance of Garreaux.

HIRAM
I presume the plans I found belonged to you.

GARREAUX
<u>Belong</u> to me, M'sieu

He extracts the plans

JOEL
What about Nuveau..?

GARREAUX
(shrugs)
Police Chiefs are easy to replace.

HIRAM
What do you intend to do?

GARREAUX
Some people search for sunken treasure, do they not?

HIRAM
Yes indeed. I'm rather an enthusiast myself.

GARREAUX
I'm going to provide them with the greatest treasure of all.

HIRAM
Really?

GARREAUX
Yes, you.

HIRAM
Well now.

GARREAUX
Do you not find that a good jest?

HIRAM
Excellent. Although I'm not entirely certain future treasure hunters will appreciate it.

GARREAUX
I am not concerned. Let us go.

He herds Hiram and Joel out the door.

OIL DISSOLVE TO:

INT. CABIN - DAY - FULL SHOT

GARREAUX
(in a state of shock)
So he is gone. At last I am rid of Hiram Holliday.

JOEL
(vehement)
No you're not. Even if he is dead, you'll never be rid of him

GARREAUX
I will be rid of him. Won't I, Marlene?

MARLENE
Of course.

JOEL
He'll come back and haunt you. He'll make life miserable.

GARREAUX
(drawing himself up) No. He will not.

MARLENE
What about him, Garreaux?

GARREAUX
Once the transfer has been made, I will dispose of him.

JOEL
Remember what I said, Garreaux. You'll never be rid of Hiram Holliday.

GARREAUX
Come, Marlene.

They exit the cabin.

DISSOLVE TO:

EXT. OCEAN - DAY - STOCK SHOT - HIRAM

As he surfaces and looks around.

(STOCK SHOT FROM ADV. OF SEA CUCUMBER)

POV SHOT - THE YACHT - (STOCK) STOCK SHOT HIRAM
As he dives under again (SEA CUCUMBER)

DISSOLVE TO:

INT. GARREAUX'S CABIN - NIGHT - TWO SHOT - GARREAUX AND MARLENE

Marlene is primping, as Garreaux paces the room.

MARLENE
Relax, Garreaux. The submarine will be here soon.

GARREAUX
It is not that. I feel him. He is on this ship!

Marlene whirls on Garreaux.

MARLENE
Hiram Holliday is at the bottom of the sea!

GARREAUX
No. His body, yes. His memory -- no! It is here, on this ship.

MARLENE
It is in your head!

GARREAUX
Yes. I am sick. I must walk about the deck. To forget him.

CUT TO:

EXT. DECK - DAY - MED. SHOT - HIRAM

As he clambers aboard and looks around speculatively.

MED. SHOT - GARREAUX

As he comes up the deck, then reacts, wide-eyed.

ANOTHER ANGLE - HIRAM AND GARREAUX

GARREAUX
No!

HIRAM
How do you do?

GARREAUX
It is true! You have come back to haunt me! You are a ghost.

HIRAM
Yes. I am a ghost. I have come back to haunt you.

GARREAUX
(proudly)
You will not succeed

HIRAM
No?

GARREAUX
(he sinks)
You will succeed

A nearby cabin door opens in the b.g., and Joel looks out. CLOSE SHOT - JOEL
He reacts, big.

MED. SHOT - GARREAUX, HIRAM AND JOEL

Joel is in the b.g. listening.

HIRAM
Give me the plans and release Joel. Then I will go away. I will not haunt you any more.

GARREAUX
No! You will never go away!

Joel moves up to Garreaux.

JOEL
Garreaux! What's the matter? Are you sick?

GARREAUX
(pointing at Hiram) Look! He is back!

JOEL
(looks around) Who's back?

GARREAUX
Hiram Holliday? Do you not see him?

JOEL
I don't see anything. You'd better go lie down for a while.

GARREAUX
Yes. I will lie down for a while.

He moves away, shaking his head in bewilderment. The CAMERA MOVES IN on Hiram and Joel.

JOEL
Hiram, how'd you get out?

HIRAM
It wasn't easy Joel.

JOEL
Those chains, and locks...

HIRAM
An escape artist named Rabatini used to warm up in a trunk like that, Joel. He once showed me how it's done.

JOEL
I knew you'd be back!
(a slight pause)
But now what do we do? We're in the middle of the ocean!

HIRAM
You're quite right. We'd best repair to your cabin for a bit of strategy.

They move toward Joel's cabin.

CUT TO:

INT. GARREAUX'S CABIN - DAY - FULL SHOT

Marlene is still in the cabin, as Garreaux bursts through the door.

MARLENE
Is it over? The Hiram Holliday disease?

GARREAUX
I saw him. And I talked to him. He has come back.

MARLENE
What? It is impossible for him to have escaped!

GARREAUX
His ghost, Marlene, has escaped.

MARLENE
Ghosts! If you saw Hiram Holliday he is no ghost!

She starts for the door.

GARREAUX
Where are you going?

MARLENE
(seductively)
To capture the ghostly Hiram Holliday

She moves out, Garreaux following.

INT. CABIN - DAY - MED SHOT - HIRAM AND JOEL

JOEL
If there were only some way we could radio shore!

HIRAM
I doubt it would do much good.

JOEL
Why not?

HIRAM
If I know Garreaux, he's got the entire island of Tahiti on his payroll.

Joel begins to pace the room, when the door opens and Marlene enters, followed by a timid Garreaux.

MARLENE
So!

GARREAUX
See! There he is!

JOEL
Sure, I'm here. Where'd you expect me to be?

GARREAUX
No, Hiram Holliday!!
(to Marlene)
Do you see him?

MARLENE
(smiles at Hiram) I see him.

JOEL
(desperately)
Don't tell me you're haunted by him too?

MARLENE
Yes. I am haunted.

She moves towards Hiram, backing him into a corner.

CLOSE ANGLE - HIRAM AND MARLENE
As she circles her arms about his neck.

HIRAM
(nervously)
Please...

MARLENE
You are a warm ghost...

HIRAM
(pointing downward)
My new surroundings. I had rather expected to go the other way...

MARLENE
Give Marlene a kiss, Hiram.

She gives one to him. They break apart, and Marlene backs off.

HIRAM
You certainly are getting into the "spirit" of things...

He laughs nervously.

MARLENE
(to Garreaux)
He is no ghost, Garreaux!

GARREAUX
You are right! He is alive.

HIRAM
Can I dare hope that might be a reasonably permanent condition?

GARREAUX
(draws his gun) It is most temporary

Marlene, standing by a porthole, reacts.

MARLENE
Garreaux, the submarine! It is here.

Garreaux moves to the window, and looks outside.

POV SHOT - SUBMARINE - (STOCK)
Surfacing (USE STOCK FROM PILOT)
MED SHOT - GROUP

GARREAUX
You will excuse me, gentlemen. I shall deal with you later.

He and Marlene exit.

THE ADVENTURE OF THE TREASURE TROVE

EXT. DECK - DAY - MED. SHOT - GARREAUX AND MARLENE

As they exit the cabin and Garreaux locks the door. They move toward the rail to greet the submarine captain, STRIKER, as he comes aboard the ship.

STRIKER
Garreaux

GARREAUX
Captain Striker

STRIKER
Mademoiselle

MARLENE
Captain

STRIKER
(to Garreaux)
You have the plans?

GARREAUX
I am Garreaux

He hands the papers to Striker, who looks them over carefully.

STRIKER
Hmm. These plans call for the torpedoing of an aircraft carrier.

GARREAUX
(nodding)
It is the first step. The carrier floats but moments from here.

STRIKER
I did not realise it would include this.

GARREAUX
You have torpedoes?

STRIKER
Of course.

GARREAUX
Then the carrier presents no problem.

STRIKER
I suppose not.

GARREAUX
I shall meet you in your vessel in a moment. There is someone I wish to bring along.

Garreaux smiles and moves out as Striker and Marlene look after him quizzically.

DISSOLVE TO:

INT. TORPEDO CHAMBER - DAY - MED SHOT - GARREAUX, STRIKER AND CREWMAN

As Garreaux smiles at something at a lower angle o.s.

GARREAUX
Excellent.

STRIKER
You are a madman Garreaux.

GARREAUX
Perhaps you are right. But it makes me happy.

ANOTHER ANGLE

Revealing the torpedo, waiting to be loaded. Hiram is strapped to the torpedo.

HIRAM
I get the feeling, Garreaux, that you don't want me around.

GARREAUX
Nonsense. You are my friend.

HIRAM
Really? Do you think you could arrange to make me an enemy?

Striker, at the periscope, reacts.

STRIKER
There it is.

Garreaux moves to the periscope.

POV - CARRIER
Seen through the periscope.
MED. SHOT - THE GROUP
As Garreaux reacts, pleased.

GARREAUX
(to Striker)
You are prepared to fire?

STRIKER
Yes.

GARREAUX
Then proceed.

STRIKER
(to crewman) Load torpedo!

The crewman moves to the torpedo and begins to slide it toward the open chamber.

HIRAM
You're quite sure I won't slow it down?

GARREAUX
Quite. Adieu, Hiram Holliday. A pleasant trip.

HIRAM
Thank you.

The crewman loads the torpedo and slams the chamber door shut.

POV SHOT - THE CARRIER -(STOCK)

Through periscope

MED. SHOT
Striker at the periscope

STRIKER
Fire!

The crewman fires the torpedo.

GARREAUX
At last! He is gone!

POV SHOT - THE TORPEDO - (STOCK)

As the wake is seen through the periscope

MED. SHOT - GARREAUX
As he pushes Striker away from the 'scope.

GARREAUX (CONT'D)
I must watch.

He watches for a moment, then reacts.

STRIKER
What is it?

GARREAUX
The torpedo! It's turning around.

STRIKER
What?

GARREAUX
It's coming this way!

STRIKER
Let me see!

Striker moves to the 'scope.

POV SHOT - THE TORPEDO - (STOCK)
Coming back toward the submarine
MED. SHOT - STRIKER AND GARREAUX

GARREAUX
He would kill himself?

STRIKER
And us with him! Fool! Fool!

EXT. OCEAN - DAY - FULL SHOT - EXPLOSION -(STOCK)

As a submarine blows up.

EXT. DECK - DAY - MED. SHOT - JOEL AND MARLENE

As they both react.

JOEL
Goodbye Hiram Holliday. The bravest of the brave.

MARLENE
Goodbye Garreaux. Most foolish of the foolish!

JOEL
There will never be another Hiram Holliday, Marlene.

HIRAM
I should hope not.

ANOTHER ANGLE

To reveal Hiram, dripping wet, walking toward Joel and Marlene, who both react in complete disbelief.

HIRAM (CONT'D)
It might prove most confusing to the postal authorities.

JOEL
Hiram, you escaped!

HIRAM
Nothing to it, Joel. After I turned the torpedo around, I slipped my bonds and swam back to the yacht.

MARLENE
But you have killed Garreaux!

HIRAM
(pointing) I think not

STOCK SHOT - GROUP OF MEN

Floating in the sea, too far away to be distinguishable.

THREE SHOT - HIRAM, MARLENE AND JOEL
MARLENE
They are safe!

HIRAM
Not entirely. I'm quite sure we can find one honest policeman back on the island.

JOEL
I say leave them there to drown.

HIRAM
Joel! The Golden Rule!

Joel shakes his head, and smiles warmly.

JOEL
What can I say?

HIRAM
I believe the accepted expression, Joel, is "full speed ahead."

Hiram points o.s toward the floating men and smiles aswe

FADE OUT:

<u>TAG</u>

FADE IN:

INT. HOTEL ROOM - DAY - FULL SHOT - HIRAM AND JOEL

Joel is seated at his typewriter, as Hiram, in the b.g, struggles with an unidentifiable object.

JOEL
What a story, Hiram! Just amazing.

HIRAM
Oh, I don't know.

JOEL
Don't know? Do you realise what you did?

HIRAM
I failed to discover any sunken treasure.

JOEL
Hah! You twice pulled escape tricks that would send Houdini back to school. How many knots did you have to untie to get off the torpedo?

HIRAM
About ten. But they weren't very well tied.

JOEL
Sure. And getting out of that chest -- there must have been fifty knots and locks -- what's the matter?

Hiram rises and moves to Joel. He hands Joel a shoe, the object with which he has been struggling.

HIRAM
I seem to have knotted my shoelace, Joel. Would you give it a try?

JOEL
I, give it...?

He stops, takes the shoe, and laughs heartily as we

FADE OUT.

THE END

Index

Numbers in **bold** indicate photographs

Abbott, John 69, 72
Adams, Stanley 75, 76, 85, 114, 126, 129
Adventure in Berlin 16
"Adventure of Hiram's Holliday, The" 123-125
"Adventure of Pandora's Box, The" 133-135
"Adventure of the Amontillado, The" 129-131
"Adventure of the Attaché Case, The" 62-68, 104
"Adventure of the Christmas Fruchtbrod, The" 100-101
"Adventure of the Dancing Mouse, The" 97-100
"Adventure of the Diamond Eater, The" 129
"Adventure of the Ersatz Joel, The" 120-123
"Adventure of the False Monarch, The" 73-75, 104
"Adventure of the Gibraltar Toad, The" 81-85
"Adventure of the Hawaiian Hamzah, The" 86-90, **89**
"Adventure of the Hollow Umbrella, The" 75-77, 104
"Adventure of the Invisible Man, The" 131-133
"Adventure of the Lapidary Wheel, The" 68-72
"Adventure of the Misguided Missile, The" **44**, 58, 125-127
"Adventure of the Monaco Hermit Crab, The" 85-86
"Adventure of the Moroccan Hawk-Moth, The" 107-110, **110**
"Adventure of the Paleozoic Egg, The" 136-139
"Adventure of the Pasto Duro, The" 110-111
"Adventure of the Romantic Pigeon, The" 101-105
"Adventure of the Rustled Rocket, The" 133, 135-136
"Adventure of the Sea Cucumber, The" 77-81, 104
"Adventure of the Shipwrecked Ancestor, The" 114-117, **117**

"Adventure of the Sturmzig Cuneiform, The" 105-106
"Adventure of the Surplus General, The" 128-129
"Adventure of the Swiss Titmouse, The" 51-52, 90-94, **93**
"Adventure of the Treasure Trove, The" 133, 199-242
"Adventure of the Unkissed Bride, The" 118-120
"Adventure of the Vanishing House, The" 111-113
"Adventure of the Wrong Rembrandt, The" 94-97
Aherne, Richard 73, 75
Alderson, John 69
Allyn, William 145-146
Aloha, Lei 86
Alton, Kenneth 105
Andrews, Stella 19, 20
Arnaz, Desi 22
Askin, Leon 97
Aubuchon, Jacques 94, 96-97

Bailey, Raymond 62
Banner, John 85, 86
Baruch, Bernard 66
Beer, Jacqueline 111, 118, 120
Billboard 19-20, 32, 55
Boon, Robert 62, 118
Boone, Richard 18
Brady, John 29
Brando, Marlon 27, 66
Brown, Jared 69
Burke, Libby 30-31
Burkett, Jenifer 30-31
Bushnell, John 66

Cabot, Sebastian 78, 80-81, 107, 121
Cahan, George M 97, 99-100
Calvin, Henry 19
Capps, Anthony 80
Case, Bertha 26
Cavens, Albert 81, 86, 102
Cavens, Fred 78, 94, 102
Chandler, Joan 18
Circuit, Harold 5
Coe, Fred 19, 28
Coleman, Ed 111
Colicos, John 69, 72
Confessions of a Storyteller 4
Connelly, Marc 17
Cosmopolitan 1, 4, 6, 11, 12, 21, 40, 42, 43, 62, 67
Cosmopolitan Theatre 20-21, **21**, 23

Cox, Wally xi, 26, 27-29, 32, 33, 35, 36, 40, **40**, 41-42, 43, **44**, 44-45, 46, 47, 49, 50
    51, 53-55, **55**, 56, 57, 62, 65, 66, 67, 68, 69, 73, 75, 76, 78, 81, 85, 86, **89**, 90, 92,
    93, 93, 94, 97, 100, 102, 105, 106, 107, 111, 114, **117**, 117, 118, 121, 123, 126,
    129, 143, 144
"Crisis in London" 5-6
Cross, Ray 53
Crutcher, Robert Riley 90, 100, 101
Curtain Time 16

Daily Courier 9-10
Daily Mirror 144
Dana, Mark 78, 81, 107
Davis, Lisa 123
De Rosa, Maria 78
De Santis, Joe 111
Dean, Dizzy 3
"Death Notice in Berlin" 7-8, 16
Delevanti, Cyril 123
Dempsey, Jack 3
Doohan, James 18
Drainie, John 16
Drayton, Noel 62
Drew, Bernard 77, 80
"Duello in Rome" 8-9
Dulles, John Foster 66, 150
Dyrenforth, Harold 105

Ebel, Eric 48-50
"Enchanted Forest, The" 12
Erickson, Rod 29, 51-52, 143
Erlich, Hortense 2
Eustrel, Tony 97

Feil, Dr Georg 145
Feldary, Eric 75, 76
Firpo, Luis 3
"Flight from Vienna" 8, 9
Freeman, Donald 58, 59

Gallico, Paolo 2
Gallico, Paul xiii, 1-5, 10, 11, 12, 13, 15, 16, 20, 21, 23, 26, 40, 42, 43, 45, 62, 67, 68,
    92, 139, 145, 149
Gehrig, Lou 15
George, Tony 97
Gilbert, Doris 101, 105
Glahn, Karen 16
Goldina, Miriam 19, 20

Gomberg, Sy 30
Graff, Wilton 62, 69
Greene, Angela 73, 75
Gruskin, George 26-27, 28-29
Guinness, Alec 72, 143

Hall, Thurston 38, 62, 73, 78, 81, 86, 90, 93, 97, 102, 105
Hallack, Peggy 111
Harris, Robert H 102
Herman, Vivienne 16
Herzig, Siegfried 107, 109-110
Hicks, Russell 86
Hingert, Maureen 107, 110, **110**
Hole Jr., William H. 75, 90, 93, 94, 105, 111, 123
Hole, Jonathan 86
Hollywood Reporter, The 47, 92-93
Hunt, Marsha 21, **21**, 22-23

Irving, Hollis 102

Jiras, Bob 18
Johnson, Carlene King 121, 123
Johnson, Tor 97, 98
Jones, Bobby 3
Justine, William 97

Katch, Kurt 21, 105, 106
Kirkland, Alexander 19, 20
Kogan, Edward 18
Kohn, John 77, 80
Korper, Rene 90, 94, 100, 101
Kouznetzoff, Adia 19, 20
Kramm, Joseph A 18

Lansbury, Angela 13
Ledebur, Fredrich 118
Light, Pamela 69, 72
Lindt, Karl 102, 118

Macaulay, Richard 21
Malik, Richard 18
"Man Who Bought a Town, The" 18
Mann, Delbert 19, 20
Mariani, Joanna (Josanne) 62, 66, 94, 95
Mariscal, Alberto 111
Marks, Sherman 21
Marsac, Maurice 62, 66-67, 68

Marshall, EG 19, 20
McAvity, Thomas A. 52-53
Menken, Lawrence 15
Mercier, Louis 94
Milan, Lita 62, 67, 68, **69**, 75, 76, 94, 114, 126, 129
"Mission to Mexico" 12
Mister Peepers 28, 40, 41, 42, 43, 46, 48, 54, 58-59, 67
Moore, Ida 97
Mrs. 'Arris Goes to Paris 13
Mullally, Donn 137
Newlan, Paul 102

Nicholson, Phillip 56
Nugent, Richard see Aherne, Richard

O'Malley, J Pat 94, 97
O'Malley, John 123, 129
Patrick, Lee 123, 125
Philco Television Playhouse 18, 20, 28
Play's the Thing, The 17, 18
Poseidon Adventure, The 2, 13
Powell, Richard M. 29-31, 32, 57, 80, 105, 111, 114, 116, 118, 123, 125, 128, 129, 131, 133
Pryor, Ainslie 38, **39**, 44, 57, 62, 65, 69, 73, 75, 76, 78, 81, 85, 86, 90, 94, 95, 97, 100, 102, 105, 107, 111, 114, 118, 121, 123, 126, 129

Radio and Television Daily 117
Ralph, Eva 85, 86
Rapp, Joel 38, 107, 109, 110, 120, 145
Rapp, Paul 143, 145
Rapp, Phil 25-27, 28-29, 30, 31, 32, 38, 39-41, 45, 46, 47, 49, 50, 51, 52, 57-58, 59, 62, 66, 67-68, 69, 73, 75, 77, 80, 81, 82, 85, 86, 90, 92, 94, 97, 99, 100, 101, 107, 109, 114, 116, 117, 128, 129, 130, 131, 133, 139, 143-144, 149
Rensing, Violet 90, 93, 94, 100, 101
"Return of Hiram Holliday, The" 12
Richman, Bill 15
Rombin, Hillevi 105, 106
Rousseau, Marcel 126
Royal, Derek Parker 109

San Diego Union 58, 59
"Sanctuary in Paris" 6, 17, 18
Sanford, Ed 15
Schubert, Bernard 26, 75
Schunzel, Reinhold 18
Secret Front, The 11, 21, **21**, 23
Shapir, Ziva 97, 98, 100

Shorr, Lester 62
Simpson, Ivan F 19
Sinclair, Lister 16
Snow Goose, The 1-2, 12, 13, 15
Sonneveld, Wim 78
Sponsor 47, 52
Star Trek 18, 57, 72
Stigler, Eric 48-50
Stillman, Robert 102
"Strange War of Hiram Holliday, The" 11
Sullivan, Elliott 17, 18

"Terror Leaves Port Sheridan" 12
Thorson, Russ 86
Thyssen, Greta 100, 101
Til, Roger 97
Tonge, Philip 62
Topper 26, 30, 38, 75, 101, 109, 110, 125
Tracy, Lee 21, **21**, 22
Tracy, Spencer 16, 125
Triesault, Ivan 93
Trujillo, Rafael 67
Trujillo, Ramfis 67
Trumbo, Dalton 72
Tweed, Tommy 16

Variety 15, 67, 68, 145-146
Vye, Murvyn 78

Waller, Leon 145
Weinstein, Hannah 143, 144
Weissmuller, Johnny 3
Welles, Orson 16
Wengraf, John 73, 86, 89
Wexler, Paul 86
Whiting, Frances 12
Wilk, Max 18
Williams, Beatrice 57
Wright, Ben 69, 123, 125, 129
Wyenn, Than 107

www.ingramcontent.com/pod-product-compliance
Lightning Source LLC
Chambersburg PA
CBHW071705160426
43195CB00012B/1581